D1343142

Macmillan Computer Science Series

Consulting Editor:
Professor F.H. Sumner, University of Manchester

A. Abdellati~~f~~ M. Limame, *Oracle - A User's Guide*
Ian O ~~tion~~ *Computer Graphics Using C*
Ian ~~ffith~~, *High-resolution Computer Graphics Using FORTRAN 77*
Ian ~~Griffith~~, *High-resolution Computer Graphics Using Pascal*
M. A~~~~ *Data Types and Algorithms, second edition*
C. Bamford and F. Curran, *Data Structures, Files and Databases, second edition*
P. Beynon-Davies, *Information Systems Development, second edition*
G.M. Birtwistle, *Discrete Event Modelling on Simula*
Richard Bornat, *Understanding and Writing Compilers*
Linda E.M. Brackenbury, *Design of VLSI Systems - A Practical Introduction*
Alan Bradley, *Peripherals for Computer Systems*
G.R. Brookes and A.J. Stewart, *Introduction to occam2 on the Transputer*
P.C. Capon and P.J. Jinks, *Compiler Engineering Using Pascal*
Robert Cole, *Computer Communications, second edition*
Eric Davalo and Patrick Naïm, *Neural Networks*
S.M. Deen, *Principles and Practice of Database Systems*
C. Delannoy, *Turbo Pascal Programming*
Tim Denvir, *Introduction to Discrete Mathematics for Software Engineering*
Joyce Duncan, Lesley Rackley and Alexandria Walker, *SSADM in Practice*
D. England *et al.*, *A Sun User's Guide, second edition*
Jean Ettinger, *Programming in C++*
J.S. Florentin, *Microprogrammed Systems Design*
A.B. Fontaine and F. Barrand, *80286 and 90386 Microprocessors*
Michel Gauthier, *Ada - A Professional Course*
M.G. Hartley, M. Healey and P.G. Depledge, *Mini and Microcomputer Systems*
J.A. Hewitt and R.J. Frank, *Software Engineering in Modula-2 - An Object-oriented Approach*
Patrick Jaulent, *The 68000 - Hardware and Software*
M.J. King and J.P. Pardoe, *Program Design Using JSP - A Practical Introduction, second edition*
Bernard Leguy, *Ada - A Programmer's Introduction*
M. Léonard, *Database Design Theory*
David Lightfoot, *Formal Specification Using Z*
A.M. Lister and R.D. Eager, *Fundamentals of Operating Systems, fifth edition*
Elizabeth Lynch, *Understanding SQL*
Tom Manns and Michael Coleman, *Software Quality Assurance, second edition*
B.A.E. Meekings, T.P. Kudrycki and M.D. Soren, *A book on C, third edition*
R.J. Mitchell, *C++ Object-oriented Programming*
R.J. Mitchell, *Microcomputer Systems Using the STE Bus*
R.J. Mitchell, *Modula-2 Applied*
Y. Nishinuma and R. Espesser, *UNIX - First Contact*
Ian Pratt, *Artificial Intelligence*
Pham Thu Quang and C. Chartier-Kastler, *MERISE in Practice*
A.J. Pilavakis, *UNIX Workshop*

continued overleaf

SSADM in Practice

A Version 4 Text

Joyce Duncan, Lesley Rackley
and Alexandria Walker

MACMILLAN

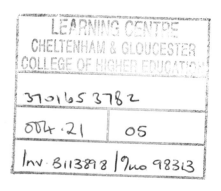
First published 1995 by
MACMILLAN PRESS LTD
Houndmills, Basingstoke, Hampshire RG21 2XS
and London
Companies and representatives
throughout the world

ISBN 0-333-46999-2

A catalogue record for this book is available
from the British Library.

Printed in Great Britain by
Antony Rowe Ltd, Chippenham, Wiltshire

Contents

Preface

This book concerns the Structured Systems Analysis and Design Method (SSADM) which was devised in the early 1980s by the Civil Service, in conjunction with LBMS (Learmonth & Burchett Management Services) to aid systems analysts in their task of developing new computer systems. SSADM was adopted as a mandatory standard by the Civil Service in 1983. Version 4 of SSADM was launched in May 1990 and it is this version that is used in this book.

The book is designed to give both an overview of SSADM for the layman and a step-by-step user guide for the aspiring practitioner. A case study is used throughout the book to provide practical examples of the techniques. This case study concerns the reservations booking requirements for a chain of hotels. A full set of SSADM documentation for this system is provided in the Appendices. It is hoped that this Case Study will provide the reader with a context in which to more clearly navigate the labyrinth of SSADM.

SSADM version 4 clearly separates the project management responsibilities from the system analysis and design activities and this book concentrates on the analysis and design tools and techniques. Reference is made to the project management area only when, it is felt by the authors, it clarifies the context of the analysis and design tasks.

The book is not intended as a learned treatise but rather a user friendly readable introduction and reference. It is written, we hope, to satisfy the needs of both educator and student in the learning of up-to-date concepts of systems analysis and design using a widely respected method.

If systems analysts are refered to as 'he' in the text of this book, it is not intended to imply that this is the normal state, merely a matter of linguistic convenience.

Acknowledgements

I would like to thank Joyce Duncan and Lesley Rackley for conceiving the idea and writing the original script and case study material. It has been my privilege to revise this original idea into SSADM version 4, also thanks to Lesley Rackley for her input to the finished script.

I would also like to thank some long suffering colleagues, Richard Skellam, Dr. Martyn Spink, Ursula Hayes and Helen Sheehy for their patience and support, Malcolm Stewart and Ian Procter for their encouragement and, on a more personal note, Pradeep Raithatha for listening.

Alexandria Walker

1 Introduction to Systems Analysis and Design

1.1 Introduction

In this chapter we look at the traditional system development life cycle, identify the problems associated with it, introduce the concept of structured methods and provide a brief introduction to the Structured Systems Analysis and Design Method (SSADM).

Our first task is to describe what we mean by the term 'systems analysis'. A business is made up of a number of functions such as accounts, marketing, production, etc. Each of these areas can be described as a subsystem of the overall business system. Similarly, each function can be further subdivided into a number of smaller subsystems, for example, invoicing, advertising, stock control, etc.

The role of a systems analyst is to critically examine the objectives of a particular subsystem, or group of subsystems, and the activities involved in achieving those objectives. The analyst's aim is to improve the efficiency and effectiveness of the business, where appropriate, through the introduction of better procedures and methods of working. These new or revised procedures may in turn be described as a system, in that they are an integrated group of activities with a common set of objectives.

1.2 Systems Development Life Cycle

Most traditional approaches to systems analysis and design specify a number of tasks which the analyst is expected to perform in a more or less sequential manner. Although the tasks are generally loosely defined and only limited guidance on their execution may be available, the process of systems analysis and design can nevertheless be thought of as a number of stages. The complete set of stages is known as the Systems Development Life Cycle (SDLC) - see Figure 1.1.

The stages involved are:
- Project definition

- Feasibility study - initial investigation and analysis

- Detailed investigation and analysis

- System design

- Program design and coding

- Implementation and review

- Maintenance

Sections 1.2.1 to 1.2.8 describe these stages in more detail.

1

It should be borne in mind that although the SDLC has been described as a set of discrete stages, in reality, the steps are not always self-contained. Additionally, some steps may be repeated in the light of subsequent findings or discussions, so the process of system development becomes iterative.

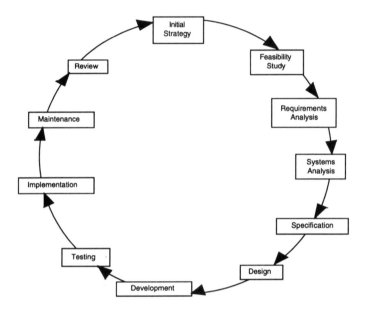

Figure 1.1 The System Development Life Cycle (SDLC)

1.2.1 Project Definition

Before a project can begin, we must establish the objectives and the areas of the business which are involved. The need to begin a new project may arise from a variety of causes. For example, it may be that the existing manual system has proved inadequate to handle a particular set of circumstances, or it may be that the requirements of an entirely new company or department need to be defined and subsequently satisfied.

The starting point for a project should be a Project Initiation Document that includes 'terms of reference'. In systems analysis, the terms of reference are usually produced jointly by the client (or user) and the analyst and define:

• The objectives and scope of the investigation or project.

• The resources available or required and the timescales involved.

• Any limitations or constraints.

This document forms the basis of a contract between the analyst and the user. It is important for both the analyst and the user to know what they are expecting to achieve before the project begins. The analyst also needs to be able to judge whether the timescale and resources that he is being allowed are realistic. Equally, should the nature of the project change as it progresses (a fairly common occurrence), it may be necessary to adjust the timescales and resource requirements accordingly.

An example of the Project Initiation Document for the case study used in this book is shown in Appendix 1.

1.2.2 Feasibility Study

Once the terms of reference have been defined, it may be necessary to carry out a feasibility study in order to decide how viable the project really is before too many resources are committed.

Within a feasibility study, a preliminary investigation, analysis and design are carried out with the aim of:

- understanding the operation of the present system and its problems

- identifying the requirements for the new system

- identifying a range of viable solutions to the problem

- identifying the cost/benefit implications involved

More specifically, the study should embrace the following:

- Overview of the current system (if appropriate)

    - objectives
    - outline description of processing
    - outline description of input and output data requirements
    - operational constraints, e.g. volumes of data, timescales for processing, etc.
    - problems, shortcomings, costs

- Requirements for the new system

    - objectives
    - overview of output, input, processing and data

- Overview of a range of alternative solutions comprising, for each solution

    - outline description
    - recommended hardware/software
    - technical feasibility, i.e. will the proposed hardware and/or software be able to solve the problem?

- are suitably qualified personnel available to develop the system?
- economic feasibility, i.e. how much will the solution cost (hardware, software, staff, training, etc.)?
- what are the benefits? can they be quantified (reduction in staff, reduction in stock levels)?
- do the benefits justify the costs?
- what are the risks of implementing the system (e.g. financial loss)?
- what is the cost of not implementing the system? (e.g. loss of competitive edge)
- operational feasibility, that is -
  can the system actually be developed and implemented within the given timescales?
  what impact will the system have on the users (e.g. skill implications, retraining, redundancy, etc.)?

• overall recommendation.

- other implications. For example, if the system is to hold personal data, is the company registered under the Data Protection Act?

Some projects may be abandoned after the feasibility study has been produced for a variety of reasons. It may be too expensive to proceed with developing the new system. There may be too many political repercussions within the company. It may not be possible to get the system installed within an acceptable timescale, etc.

1.2.3 Detailed Investigation and Analysis

Assuming that the project proceeds after the feasibility study has been assessed, a detailed analysis phase is essential. The purpose of the analysis phase in the System Development Life Cycle is to understand a system by breaking it down into comprehensible units. Additionally, the analyst aims to determine what has to be done to solve any problems that he identifies in the operation of the system.

It is important to recognise that we are looking at a solution in terms of what needs to be done rather than how it will be achieved. There is a tendency for analysts who have a programming background to jump ahead into the technicalities of how before really understanding the requirements that they are trying to meet. The how of the system should generally not be addressed until the design stages of the development life cycle.

The first phase of analysis is an investigation of the current system if one exists. The main techniques used for investigation are interviewing, observation and questionnaires. The results of the investigation also need to be documented, for example using system or document flow charts, narrative description, etc.

Having discovered and documented how the current system operates, the analysis process attempts to identify

- Essential features of the existing system which need to be incorporated into the new system.

- Problems within the current system which the new system will need to solve.

- Additional requirements for the new system which the current system does not attempt to meet.

In some instances there may not be an existing system, in which case the systems analyst will concentrate on defining the requirements of the new system, again using techniques such as interviewing and questionnaires.

1.2.4 System Design

It is only after the analysis has been successfully carried out that the design of the new system can begin. One of the first set of tasks will be to decide how the data will be put into the system and what form the data coming out of the system will take. This will then lead to the identification of the processing requirements and the data storage needed within the system to meet the input and output requirements. Audit, security and control procedures should also be considered at this point in development.

The result of this stage of the System Design Life Cycle is the production of a detailed document, or specification. In some installations the specification of the processing is so detailed, that no further refinements to the program design are required. In other cases, the specification is only an outline and further program design and specification has to be carried out.

1.2.5 Program Design and Coding

It is the job of the programming team to produce all of the programs required for the system. The method used in the design of the programs will vary from installation to installation depending, for example, on whether structured methods for program design are followed. Once designed, these programs need to be coded and then tested, both individually, and as a complete suite, before the implementation stage.

This separation of tasks applies particularly to the development of a system using 3rd generation languages and conventional file handling languages such as COBOL. However, with the availability of 4th generation languages, applications generators, etc. the amount of coding, and even the need for specialist coders, is diminishing.

1.2.6 Implementation

A number of activities are covered by this phase:

- System testing. The system has to be thoroughly tested to ensure that it satisfies all of the user requirements and produces the correct results.

- Establishment of the 'going live' date.

- Preparation of accommodation, hardware acquisition and installation..

- File conversion. Before the system can be fully used, existing data will have to be entered into the computer system.

- Preparation of user (and operator) manuals.

- User training.

- Change-over to the new system. This may be via parallel running, where the old and new systems are run side by side, or by direct/immediate change-over. Additionally, in the case of large systems, the change-over may need to be phased, e.g. office by office, facility by facility.

A post-implementation review should be carried out about six months after implementation. The aim of this review is to review the success of the project in terms of the system performance; for example, whether the timing metrics are being achieved, if data correctness and integrity are being maintained, are the security measures being correctly implemented and working and most importantly is the system meeting the user's requirements? The answers to these and other related questions will establish whether any changes are needed and to determine what lessons, if any, should be learnt for the benefit of future projects.

1.2.7 Maintenance

The term 'maintenance' covers enhancements and improvements to the system, as well as the correction of any errors. Although thorough testing of the system should have been carried out, it is possible that a particular sequence of events or an unusual set of data may trigger errors long after the implementation of the system. Additionally, new requirements which were not foreseen may surface at a later date. If the analyst has made the system design too rigid then a major redesign may be required to update the system, and this may prove very expensive in staff costs. Consequently, it is particularly important to ensure that systems are designed with the possibility of change in mind.

1.2.8 Project Evaluation Review

As part of the final stage of the project there may be a 'Project Evaluation Review'. This will be carried out to assess the project management, how effectively the management plan was carried out and if the plan itself was successful in controlling and managing the project.

1.3 Structured Systems Analysis and Design

A structured method of analysis and design is one which gives the analyst a set of well-defined tasks to carry out in a specific order, together with a range of appropriate tools and techniques. Checkpoints may be included at the end of one or more tasks to review the results to date and to ensure that the user and analyst are in agreement with such results. The major features of traditional and structured methods are contrasted in Table 1.2.

Table 1.2 - Comparison of Traditional and Structured Methods

Traditional Methods	Structured Methods
Broad guidelines	Detailed step by step procedures
Variety of individual tools and techniques	Wider range of integrated tools and techniques
Add-on documentation	Integrated documentation
Limited capability for automation	Capable of at least partial automation

1.3.1 Why Use a Structured Method?

Many large organisations have adopted structured methods of analysis and design with a view to tackling a range of problems not solved by 'traditional' approaches to system development. These problems can be categorised roughly into those concerned with quality of design and those concerned with maintainability.

1.3.2 Quality of Design

When assessing the quality of a quality design, the first question that arises is 'Does the computer system do what the user wants it to do?' All too frequently the answer to this question is 'No'. Such a major shortcoming may arise for a number of reasons. One possible cause is a lack of communication between analyst and user.

Structured methods aim to improve such communication by offering a standard approach to analysis and design and a standard set of diagramming techniques for the presentation of information. During the analysis phase the user requirements are documented in a requirements catalogue of some form (sometimes referred to as requirements capture). Additionally, some methods include a series of reviews where the work completed so far must be 'signed off' as approved by the client before the next stage can be started. This ensures firstly that the analyst and client/user are in agreement regarding the problems to be solved and, secondly, that the user actively participates in the analysis and design activities.

Another major cause of poorly designed computer systems is the tendency amongst many systems analysts to start designing the system before the analysis is finished. This may mean that a design created in such a way may not reflect the real requirements of the client as they may not all be discovered. It may also mean that the system is not designed to meet the client requirements but to fit in with the ideas that the analyst has already developed in terms of hardware, software, etc. Structured methods on the other hand ensure that the analysis stages are completed before the design is attempted. Additionally, the early stages of design can be undertaken without being constrained by consideration of any hardware or software implications. This means that the designer can concentrate on what the system should do, rather than how this will be achieved.

1.3.3 Maintainability

The use of a standard method is in itself a major aid to the task of maintenance. By providing guidelines for the development of a system and standard documentation, structured methods ensure that staff not originally involved in the project team and even relatively newly trained analysts can easily understand and maintain a system.

Inadequate documentation can mean that the analyst and/or programmer spends a long time trying to understand how the current system works before any amendments can be implemented. If an unstructured method is used, documentation may well be left until the end of the project or never be done at all. In structured methods comprehensive and up-to-date documentation is produced as the project progresses and thus the development of the project, as well as the final system, is recorded for the benefit of the maintenance team.

Another commonly encountered maintenance problem is a design which proves difficult to adapt as user needs alter. Unstructured methods allow the analyst to define the data and processing activities together, so that if processing requirements change, the data may also need to be changed. Structured methods, on the other hand, demand thorough analysis of the properties of the data independently of the identified current processing needs and of the eventual file or database design. This gives a flexibility that reflects the real world needs of business environments, where data itself is unlikely to change but processing requirements may be changing all the time.

1.3.4 User Involvement

Structured analysis and design methods have formalised the involvement of users in the development of new systems through the use of reviews, as described in section 1.3.2. Many so-called 'traditional' analysts would argue that they have always involved the user and indeed that it is impossible not to do so when designing a product to meet his needs. Nevertheless there are a good many dissatisfied clients who say that their analyst's idea of involvement was a reluctant once-per-month debriefing session.

The user's primary concern is in how the system is going to be presented to them, what menu structure, ease of movement between the menus, the format, content and significance of reports and documents, etc. As users they are generally not interested, and have no need to be involved, in how the programs are going to achieve the end results; however, it has been found that by involving the user in the development cycle they show a greater sense of ownership of the completed system. In SSADM this has been recognised and a series of 'user reviews' take place throughout the development cycle.

Three limitations however still apply to user involvement. Firstly, in order to participate, the user must understand the techniques and diagrams that are presented to him. (For this reason many clients attend a brief training course to acquaint themselves with the structured method.) Secondly, the reviews may become a substitute for full user participation by being the only points at which users are consulted. Thirdly, if a user does not wish to be involved in the development process, or if an analyst is determined to exclude or mystify the client, it is difficult to enforce user involvement in its full sense. However, a general trend that is emerging, whether using structured or unstructured methods, is for the user to become a full member of the project team and to play an active role throughout the project life cycle.

1.4 Structured Systems Analysis and Design Methodology (SSADM)

SSADM is one of the most widely used structured methods of analysis and design in the public and private sector of business in Britain.

An overview of the main features of SSADM is given later in this chapter. In essence the method consists of the following :

- SSADM Version 4 provides a framework of procedures that produce the required products for each stage of system development and sits neatly inside an all-encompassing shell of project management (See Figure 1.3).

- A range of tools and techniques for use by the analyst/designer.

- A set of documentation for the final system which also shows how the system has developed throughout the analysis and design phases.

A diagram to illustrate how the stages of SSADM Version 4 maps onto the SDLC phases is shown in Figure 1.5 on Page 13.

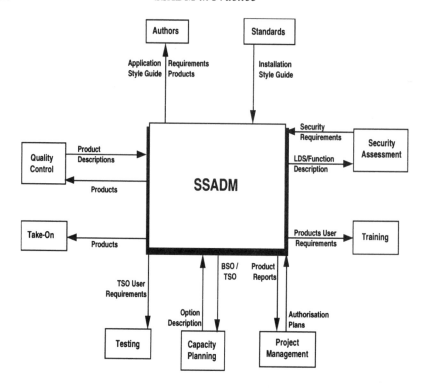

Figure 1.3 : The SSADM Framework

1.4.1 Principles of SSADM

SSADM is based on a number of key principles:

- An iterative approach to analysis and design. This involves the steps being repeated as and when necessary to ensure that the analysis is correct and complete.

- A 'top-down' approach which allows the analyst to gain an overview of the system before concentrating on the finer detail.

- Separation of 'logical' design (what the system will do) from the 'physical' design (how it will be achieved). This separation allows the analyst the freedom to develop the system without having to consider, in the initial stages, the constraints imposed by specific hardware and software.

- Three views of the system, in terms of:

  - The structure of the data

  - The way in which the data is moved round the system

- The way that data changes through time, together with the sequence of events which cause the changes.

Using three separate approaches to the design of the system ensures a degree of cross-checking.

- A data-driven approach in that the structure of the system is held to be largely determined by the structure of the data. In other words, although the user's processing requirements may change over time, the underlying data structure should remain unaltered. Assuming that this data structure has been correctly determined, processing changes should be straightforward to implement.

- Physical design guidance, where a set of rules is given for:

    - the conversion of the logical design to the physical design

    - the optimisation of the resultant data and program design.

- A full set of documentation which is produced as part of the analysis and design process.

1.4.2 Modules of SSADM

SSADM Version 4 is initially divided into modules; this aligns with the idea of making the method tailorable to specific project needs. Each module has a defined purpose and set of products. Modules have no explicit dependency on one another; however, they would be completed in a defined sequence, and the link between the modules is caused by the products from one becoming the inputs to the next. The method can be used as set out in Figure 1.4, or whole modules could be replaced with alternative procedures to suit a particular project environment.

1.4.3 Stages of SSADM

SSADM has four main modules. These four modules consist of six stages shown in Figure 1.4. These are compared with the steps in the SDLC of Figure 1.3, giving Figure 1.5. The stages themselves are subdivided into a series of steps and in each step a prescribed set of tasks is carried out. An overview of the stages is presented below. Each stage, and the techniques required to carry it out, is given a more rigorous treatment in subsequent chapters.

There is one other module/stage in SSADM version 4. Stage 0 deals with a Feasibility Study; and this is an optional activity. Consequently Stage 0 has not been explored within this book.

Stage 1 - Investigation of the current environment documents the current system (if it exists) and production of a Requirements Catalogue, data model and process model.

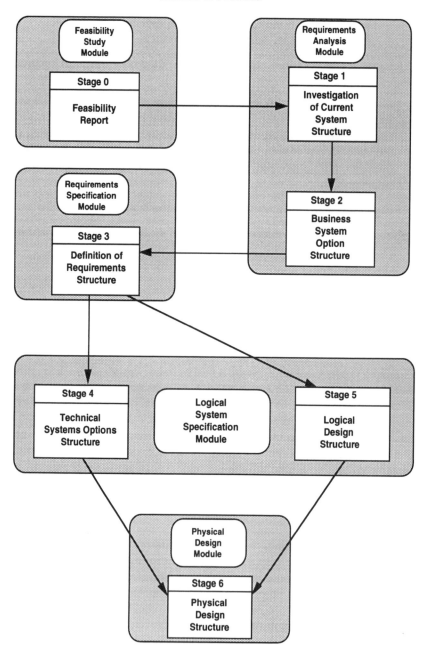

Figure 1.4 : The Modules and Stages of SSADM

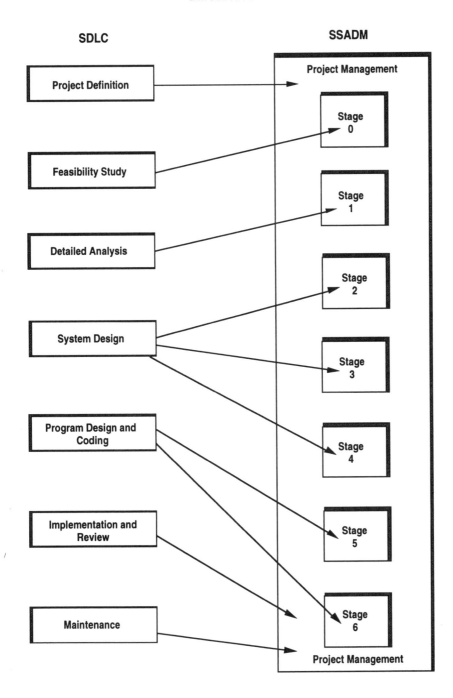

Figure 1.5 : SDLC mapped to SSADM Stages

Stage 2   Provides User Management with prepared options (Business System Options) describing the scope and functionality of alternative ways of developing a system to meet their requirements.

Stage 3   Definition of Requirements takes the selected Business System Option and refines the requirements catalogue, data and process models expanding the detail into function descriptions and Input/Output structures.

Stage 4   Technical system option is the evaluation of the best technical products to meet the requirements specification. This is carried out in parallel with

Stage 5   Logical Design, (i.e. what the new system will do) providing the detailed specification of processing structures, data and Human Computer Interfaces in the form of dialogues.

Stage 6   Physical design (i.e. how the new system will work) specifies the physical data, processes, inputs and outputs. In reality it covers everything needed to decide an application's construction and implementation methods.

1.5 Summary

In this chapter we have tried to give the reader an insight into the process of systems analysis and design, together with a brief introduction to a structured method - SSADM. In the following chapters we examine the steps and techniques involved in an SSADM project.

2 Stage 1 : Investigation of Current Environment

2.1 Overview

In this chapter we look in more detail at SSADM Stage 1 and introduce the technique of Data Flow Diagramming and the Requirements Catalogue (RC).

A diagram of the steps and tasks associated with Stage 1 is shown in Figure 2.1. In this stage, the analyst is concerned with finding out how the present system or area of the business operates, and gaining an understanding of all those who have an interest in the system and their objectives. This involves the traditional analysis skill of information gathering.

Detailed requirements are collected and models of the business are built to reflect these findings using detailed Data Flow Diagrams (DFDs), Logical Data Model (LDM), Requirements Catalogue (RC) and User Catalogue (UC).

These physical views will then be converted to a logical view to produce a comprehensive survey result that ignores the physical constraints. These constraints and related problems will be recorded with other system objectives in the RC.

2.2 Establish Analysis Framework (Step 110)

The objectives of this step are to review the Project Initiation Document (Terms of Reference) and any previous studies, e.g. Feasibility Study, to identify system requirements, to confirm the system scope and boundaries and to create detailed plans for the investigation process. The Project Initiation Document for our case study hotel system is shown in Appendix 1.2.

As the name of this step implies this is principally concerned with the preparation for detailed analysis. The Terms of Reference will provide the initial entries in the RC, while the review of documentation determines the boundaries and is formalised as a model using a Context Diagram.

The Terms of Reference, RC and Context Diagram will then be used to create an initial Level 1 Data Flow Diagram and an Overview Logical Data Structure to provide a system model for use in the subsequent steps of detailed analysis.

2.2.1 The Requirements Catalogue

Requirements generally consist of a collection of problems which have been identified in the current system, together with a set of requirements for the new system. An example of part of the RC for the Hotel System is shown in Appendix 7.

The terms of reference provide a starting point for the RC which is expanded during production of the current system Data Flow Diagrams (DFDs), and may

15

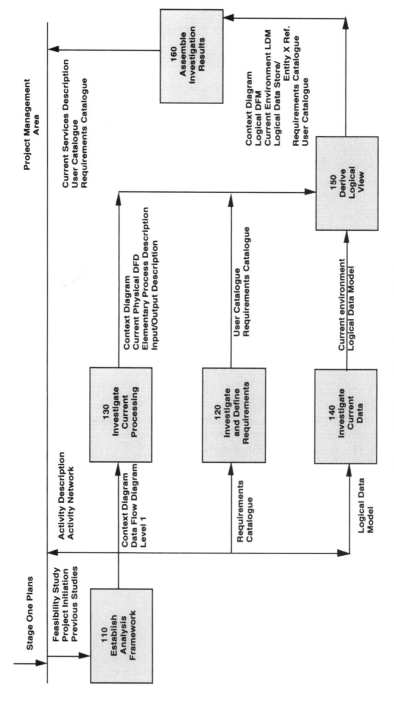

Figure 2.1 Stage One Steps and Products

be further modified during the development of the Logical Data Structure (LDS). It is important to be as specific as possible in defining requirements so that subsequent misinterpretations can be avoided. Although this may be difficult in the first instance, a clearer picture should emerge as the analysis proceeds, enabling the degree of precision to be gradually increased. It must also be remembered that the requirements should be stated in terms of the business needs and not in terms of how these needs might be met and that acceptance criteria for requirements should be in measurable, testable terms (see the example cited in section 2.3). As the problems and requirements tend to be entered in an ad hoc manner by different members of the team, it is important to review and consolidate entries periodically; it may be, for example, that one person's problem is another's requirement. The RC is formally reviewed with the client at the end of Stage1 (and again during Stage2); it is a product that is constantly under review as the project progresses.

2.2.2 Context Diagram

The context diagram shows the entire system as a single process with all the flows from external entities and to recipients (also shown as external entities). This diagram helps to define the system boundaries; this assists in planning the investigation. An example of a context diagram will be found in Appendix 2.

2.3 Detailed Investigation of the Current System (Steps 120, 130, 140)

The three steps involved are carried out in parallel

- Step 120 - Investigation and Definition of Requirements

- Step 130 - Investigation of Current Processing

- Step 140 - Investigation of Current Data

Having established the terms of reference, the analyst will then proceed to investigate the current system following the plan developed in Step 110. In Stage 1 of SSADM, he is building up a picture of the current physical system, that is, the way in which the current system operates, such as: who does what (User Catalogue Section 5.2.7), what records are kept, what timescales are involved, how much data is needed, etc., (Data Catalogue, Input/Output Descriptions, Section 2.4.7). In other words, he is looking not only at what is done, but how it is done. At the same time, the analyst is beginning to identify the problems that the business is encountering and to suggest ways in which some of the objectives stated in the terms of reference can be turned into specific practical requirements. For example, the request,'management information to be available more quickly', becomes, 'occupancy figures should be provided for each hotel on a weekly basis and should be available to regional and central headquarters within 24 hours of the end of the week (Sunday)'.

During the investigation, the analyst will be producing Data Flow Diagrams (see 2.4) and a Logical Data Model (LDM, see Chapter 3) to record and represent the current system. Additionally, these techniques will aid him with his analysis by revealing any omissions in his knowledge of the working of the business and by highlighting inefficiencies, such as the duplication of the same data across a number of files.

If there is no existing system to investigate, the analyst will proceed straight to stage 2 having entered the requirements (from the terms of reference) on to the Requirements Catalogue (RC).

2.4 Data Flow Diagrams - Part 1 (Steps 110, 130)

Data Flow Diagrams (DFDs) are developed in Stages 1, 2 and 3 of SSADM during the analysis phase of the development of a system. They show how data enters the system, the processes which operate on that data and the storage areas in which data is held within the system. DFDs present a snapshot view of the data flowing through the system at any moment in time. They do not show the sequence in which processes are performed. In this respect they differ from flowcharts, which focus on the processes carried out in a system and the order in which these processes occur.

2.4.1 Uses of DFDs

During Stage 1 of SSADM, DFDs are used to show the way in which the current system operates. Initially, a top level (Level 1) DFD is produced giving an overview of the data and processes involved in the current system (Figure 2.2). This follows the top-down approach used in SSADM and ensures that the analyst gains an overall understanding of the system and its environment before he begins to focus on specific aspects in more depth.

In order to understand the system in more detail lower level DFDs are then produced. These are formed by expanding each of the process boxes on the higher level (Level 1) DFD into a lower level (Level 2) DFD (see the example in Figure 2.3; the remaining Level 2 DFDs for the case study are shown in Appendix 3). If necessary these may be expanded yet again to produce third-level DFDs. At this point the analyst has a set of DFDs representing the current physical system. To remind ourselves of what we mean by physical system all the data stores, processes, etc., that are used in the system at present are shown on the DFD, irrespective of their necessity or efficiency. In other words we are representing how the current system meets the user requirements. The analyst should continually review his DFDs with the user to ensure that they are correct. In practice the DFDs may need to be redrawn frequently as the analyst clarifies his understanding of the system; for this reason, some automated aid to diagramming will prove invaluable.

The Level 1 DFD for the current Hotel System (Figure 2.2) and an explanation of the symbols used follow below. A description is then provided of the steps involved in producing a Level 1 and a Level 2 DFD.

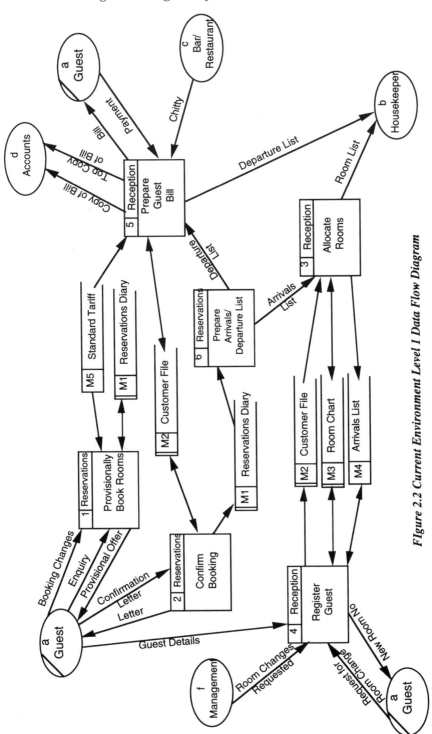

FIgure 2.2 Current Environment Level 1 Data Flow Diagram

2.4.2 Description of a Data Flow Diagram

• Dataflows can take a variety of physical forms, e.g. telephone calls, memos, forms, etc. They are shown in a DFD as a straight line, labelled with the name of the data.

• All activities or processes in a system are represented in a rectangular box. The description of the process should be as precise as possible, e.g. 'process enquiries' should be changed to a more specific explanation, such as 'check room availability'.

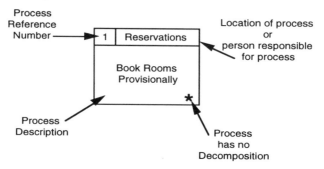

Example of a Process Box

• All data stores are shown by a narrow elongated rectangle with an open end. Any data which is kept in the system, either temporarily or permanently, is held in a data store. A data store in a system may take many physical forms, e.g. a section in a filing cabinet, a card box, an in-tray, a computer file.

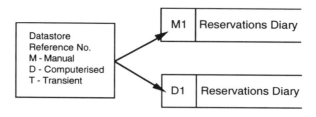

Data Store Notation

• Arrows are used to show how data is put into or taken out of data stores, e.g.

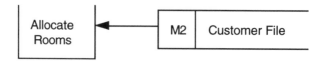

Process Reading Data Store

Process Writing to Data Store

Process Reading and Writing to Data Store

(In a Level 2 DFD, it is desirable to show the writing and reading dataflows as two separately labelled flows for the sake of completeness and clarity.)

• In order to make the DFD easier to read and to avoid crossing lines, the same data store may be drawn more than once in a DFD. Double lines indicate that this store is repeated at least once on the diagram.

Convention for duplicated data store

• The system boundary defines the area of the business which the user and the analyst have agreed should be investigated. The boundary can be indicated by a dotted line around the appropriate processes in the Level 1 DFD, although in practice it is frequently omitted.

• External entities are people, departments, etc., which receive data from, or send data into, the system, but do not carry out any processing within the system. This does not necessarily imply that they do not, for example, subsequently process data produced from the system. Any such processes are, however, outside the defined system boundary and hence are of no interest in the investigation. External entities are shown as ellipses and may be drawn more than once to aid clarity.

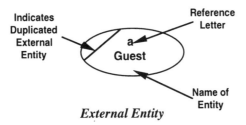

External Entity

- Occasionally clarity may be improved by showing the flow of physical items as well as the flow of data. Such movement of physical goods is shown by a large arrow containing a description of the goods. This symbol is however rarely used as the purpose of DFDs is to show the flow of data, rather than goods, within a system.

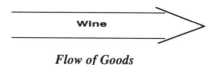

Flow of Goods

2.4.3 Steps in Producing a Level 1 DFD of the Current Physical System

Diagrams are only useful as a tool if they are clear and comprehensible. In the specific case of a DFD these criteria are unlikely to be met if there are too many process boxes. Therefore, approximately 7 should be the target. Each process box should be suitable for expanding into a Level 2 DFD. Error and exceptions handling are usually only shown on Level 2 DFDs in order to avoid complicating the overview presented in a Level 1 DFD.

A number of approaches can be adopted when producing a Level 1 DFD. Two such approaches are described below and two more are briefly mentioned.

Approach 1

- Identify the major data flows into and out of the system, together with their respective starting and finishing points (the source and recipient of the data). The source and recipient will normally become external entities on the DFD.
- Identify the processes which receive the incoming data and the stores used to hold such data.

Input Flows	Source	Receiving process	Stores used
Enquiries	Guest	Book Rooms Provisionally	Reservation Diary Standard Tariff

- Identify the processes which generate outward flows together with the relevant data stores, for example

Output Flows	Recipient	Generating process	Stores used
Bill	Guest Accounts	Prepare guest bills	Standard tariff Customer file
Daily rooms list	Housekeeper	Allocate rooms	Room details Arrivals list

- Draw a DFD showing these external entities, processes, data flows and stores.
- Add any additional processes, flows and data stores needed to link the existing processes together or to cover other activities identified during the investigation.
- Review for accuracy, completeness, etc.

Approach 2

- List the documents used in and produced by the system

> Confirmation letter
> Arrivals list
> Departure list
> Daily room list
> Bill
> Enquiries (although not necessarily a document, this is neverthe less a key information flow in the system)
> Chitty

- Identify the source and recipient of each document and construct a physical document flow diagram showing the sources and recipients as external entities (duplicated if necessary to improve clarity).

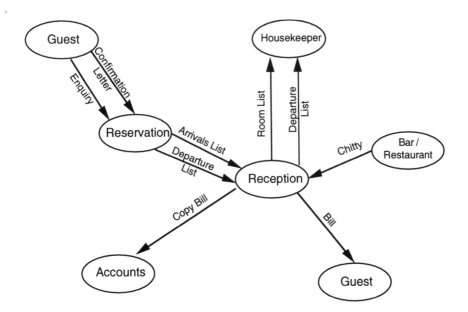

Physical Document Flow Diagram

• Review the system with the user to agree system boundary. At this stage it may also be useful to produce a Level 0 DFD, or 'context diagram' showing the system as one central process sending and receiving data to/from the external entities identified.

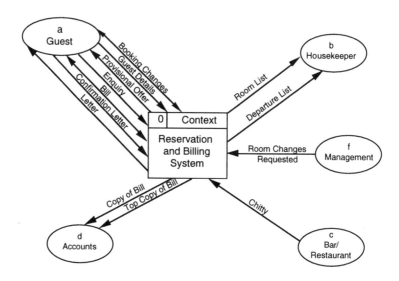

Context or Level 0 Diagram

• Identify the processes associated with each entity inside the boundary. For each key document that crosses the system boundary, identify the receiving or generating process(es) and the data stores used. Add any further data stores, data flows and processes that are necessary.

Approach 3

• Draw a number of partial DFDs, for example, for each function within the system, and then link these together.

Approach 4

• Draw a separate flow diagram for each major document in the system, showing processes, stores and external entities involved, and then link these together.

2.4.4 Low Level Data Flow Diagrams

• The Level 2 DFD in Figure 2.3 is an expansion of process 5 of the Level 1 DFD in Figure 2.2. The number and title of the Level 5 process is shown as a heading in the enlarged process box.

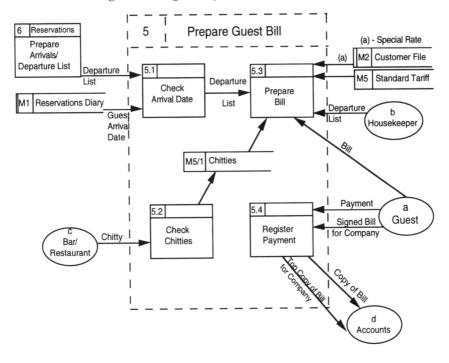

Figure 2.3 : Level 2 DFD for Process 5

• Level 2 process reference numbers are subdivisions of the Level 1 process number.

• Data stores which appear at Level 1 or in other processes are shown outside the boundary of the Level 2 process box.

• Data stores used by the Level 2 process only, are shown inside the Level 2 process box and are numbered as subordinates of the Level 2 process. These are called private data stores.

• External entities are shown outside the main level 2 process box.

• All flows identified in the Level 1 DFD must be shown on the Level 2 DFD. These flows are shown crossing the boundary of the Level 2 box. As the Level 2 is an expansion of Level 1, extra flow lines or expanded descriptions may be required to give a more detailed picture.

• Data flows, data stores and external entities may be broken down into more detail within the Level 2 DFD. For example:

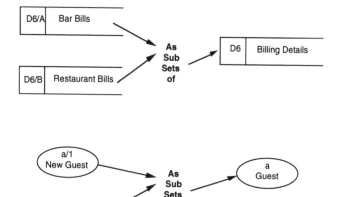

Subdivisions of Data stores and Entities

2.4.5 Steps in Producing Lower Level DFDs for the Current Physical System

A Level 2 DFD will normally have between 4 and 8 process boxes, plus possibly 4 to 8 process boxes handling errors and exceptions.

To produce the Level 2 DFDs:

- Draw a large box containing the reference number and title of the level 1 process.

- Draw the data flows into the process from the Level 1 DFD as flows crossing the boundary of the Level 2 box.

- Add the source or recipients of such flows from the Level 1 DFD.

- Identify the processes receiving or generating the flows (as for Level 1 DFDs), breaking down the flows, datastores, etc., as necessary.

- Add any additional processes, flows, stores, etc., as in the Level 1 DFD. Level 2 DFDs may also show error handling and processing of exceptions. Review against the higher level DFD and with the user.

- Examine the Level 2 DFDs to see whether any Level 3 DFDs are required.

Level Three Level 3 DFDs are rarely required unless a Level 2 diagram proves particularly complex. If several Level 1 processes need expansion to 3 levels of detail and other processes need no expansion, it may indicate that the top level DFD may need to be redrawn!

N.B. If required, Level 3 DFDs should have between 4 and 8 process boxes. The numbering follows the same convention as in Level 2 diagrams, with one more decimal point being added.

- The processes in the lowest level DFDs may need to be described by an Elementary Process Description (see 2.5).

- Other documentation which may be held in the data dictionary and which is produced while drawing the DFDs is as follows:

    The name and a description of each external entity.
    The name of each data flow and the data items making up that data flow.
    The name of each data store and a list of the data items held in the data store.

2.4.7 Validation of Data Flow Diagrams

Check the DFDs according to the following guidelines:

- Does every processes have a trigger? All processes should be started by receipt of data from an external entity or another process, or by a time event, or by an internal change (e.g. minimum stock level reached).

- Is a process triggered immediately by a previous process? If it is, the DFD should show the link as illustrated in (a). If however process x stores the data that it produces and process y subsequently uses that stored data, the DFD should be drawn as in (b).

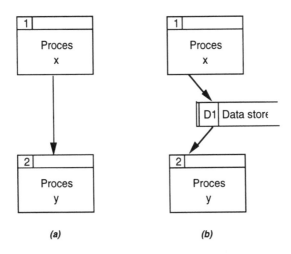

(a)   (b)

- Can the data coming out of a data store be derived from the data being put into that store? If not, how does the additional data get into that store?

- Does the data coming out of a process match the data going into it? If not, where does the additional data come from? (e.g. a data store).

- Are all data stores in the system created and deleted? If not, is it known how their creation and deletion occurs?

- Are all the data stores which are created subsequently used or modified by the system? If not what is their purpose?

- Do the words describing the processes contain precise, active verbs rather than vague generalisations?

- Do any processes have too many flows (more than 4 to 5) coming into or out of them? If so, these processes may need splitting.

- Does each level of DFD have broadly the right number of process boxes? (normally between 5 and 10)

- Do any of the processes appear to receive data which then does not reappear? If so, this data should be placed in a store.

- REVIEW THE DFDs WITH THE USER. A user may spot omissions or inaccuracies in the DFDs, so it is in the analyst's interests to consult the user as early and as frequently as possible. (At a later point, the DFD will be checked against the LDS and the entity/event matrix, see Chapters 3 and 5.)

- Add any relevant problems with the current system to the RC.

2.5 Elementary Process Descriptions

Elementary Process Descriptions (EPDs) are prepared for any process that needs further clarification after the lowest level DFDs have been constructed. The DFD process descriptions can only contain a summary of the processing needed. Consequently, any complex procedures will need to be specified in more detail and the EPD is used for this purpose. There may be a project standard for the format of these descriptions; common techniques used are:

- Pseudo code

- Structured English

- Pre/Post conditions

- Decision tables

Examples of EPDs for the Case Study are shown in Appendix 2.

2.6 Input/Output Descriptions

One of the tasks in Step 130 is to record a description of each data flow crossing the system boundary. This description should include information about the external entity and process involved, and every data attribute in the flow. An example of a flow that requires this documentation is the 'Departure List' in the case study. Examples of these descriptions can be found in Appendix 2.

2.7 Conclusion

So far we have used DFDs to represent the current physical system. DFDs are also used at a number of other stages within SSADM and these uses are explained in subsequent chapters. Suffice to say that the Data Flow Diagram is one of the major products of Structured Analysis and a knowledge of the techniques involved in the development of these diagrams is of paramount importance for the analyst.

3 Stage 1 : Investigation of Current Environment (Continued)

3.1 Introduction

This chapter introduces two concepts which are used in Stage 1: Logical Data Modelling (LDM) and the Data Store/Entity Cross Reference.

Any system, manual or computerised, is composed of data and processes. Data is in itself meaningless and only becomes meaningful when placed in context; for example, the numeric character '2' only becomes meaningful when a descriptor is added, such as £, litres, etc. As there may be millions of items of data within a fairly small system, it is necessary to simplify the analysis procedure by grouping data relating to the same or similar objects, and treating it as a single entity.

An entity is an object of the real world about which information is held in a particular system. These entities may be physical or conceptual; for example, a car is a physical object which has the properties of colour, engine size, etc., whereas a department is not something you can see but it still has properties, e.g. number of staff. The properties of an entity are called attributes. Entities within a system may be related to or dependent on each other. The nature of these relationships is defined by Logical Data Modelling (LDM).

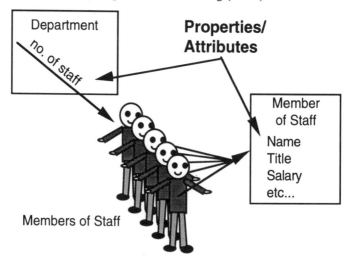

Figure 3.1 - Hidden Attributes in Entities

To put LDM into context, we know that data is moved around the system by processes. These processes may be triggered in a number of ways; for example, time, input of data from outside or from another part of the system. Data Flow

Diagrams (DFDs), introduced in Chapter 2, show how data moves around the system; LDM concentrates on the entities, or groups of data, and their relationship(s) with each other; Entity Life Histories (ELHs) identify the events which trigger the processes and show which entities in the system are created, changed or deleted by each event. (Entity Life Histories are described in detail in Chapter 7.) These three techniques allow three different views to be taken of the same system and provide a means of cross-checking the results of each technique.

3.2 Logical Data Modelling (Steps 110, 140)

Data modelling has been available to analysts for many years. There are a number of approaches to data modelling which differ only slightly from each other (e.g. entity modelling, conceptual modelling, etc.). In SSADM, the approach used is Logical Data Modelling. The aim of this technique is to:

- Identify the entities or data structures needed in the system.

- Identify the attributes (properties) of each of the entities.

- Identify the relationships between the entities and thereby the access paths to data within the system.

- Represent the entities and their relationships in diagrammatic form by means of a Logical Data Structure (LDS).

- Ultimately produce a data model which will form the basis for the final physical file or database structure.

LDM is used three times in the early stages of SSADM.

(1) In Stage 1 - Step 110 To provisionally identify the data in the current system.

(2) In Stage 1 - Step 140 To identify the data in the current system in more detail.

(3) In Stage 3 - To identify the data in the required system.

The LDM produced in Stage 3 is used in Stages 4 and 5 and then proceeds to Stage 6 possibly in a modified form.

3.3 Steps in Producing a Logical Data Structure (LDS)

3.3.1 Select Entities

We have already described an entity as an object of the real world which is relevant to a particular system. In contrast with entities in Data Flow Diagrams, which were described as being outside the system, receiving or sending data into or out of the system, entities in a logical data model are within the system itself. Although it must be remembered that the entities we are defining are logical groupings of data, not the physical forms, etc. which currently hold the data, a good starting point for identifying the entities in the current system is either the data stores in the current physical DFD or the documents within the manual system. Invoices, for example, will have various items on them, for instance customer number. If there is a customer number there is probably an entity called customer. Invoice itself may well be an entity too.

It should be noted that data stores which are purely used to hold data temporarily, probably derived from other data, should not become entities in the LDS. For example, the arrivals list in the case study is a report derived from booking details and would not constitute an entity. Equally, data stores on the DFD may contain more than one entity and entities in the current system may be duplicated across several data stores.

It is important to remember that we are considering only the 'logical' side of the system, not the 'physical' side. In other words we are interested in those distinct entities, or groups of data items which exist in the system, not how they are held. For example, although guest and booking details may be filed together in one place, they are logically different entities in that one guest may make different bookings over a period of time.

One way of clarifying 'What is an entity?' is to examine attributes (or data items) and identify those which logically belong to the same group of data. Taking the example of guest and booking, we can see that the only attribute which both have in common is 'guest name' and they therefore should be defined as two separate entities.

Although the use of Third Normal Form Analysis (TNF) is optional in Version 4 of SSADM, in practice it has been found useful as early as Stage 1 as an aid to the identification of groups of data and hence entities of the system. However, as TNF not is formally used until Stage 3 of the method, the description of the technique has been deferred until Chapter 6.

3.3.2 Investigate Interrelationships

Having identified the entities within the system, the next step is to examine the relationship between each entity and the others in the system. Although all the entities in the system may be indirectly related to each other, LDM is only concerned with direct relationships. For example, a child is directly related to his parents and the parents, in turn, are directly related to their parents. The child, however, is only indirectly related to the grandparents, that is, only through the relationship with the parent.

3.3.3 Produce a Logical Data Structure Matrix

It is sometimes difficult to decide whether a relationship is really direct or whether the relationship requires an intermediate entity to complete it. It is suggested that a matrix is created initially to help clarify the problem (see Figure 3.1). Each of the possible entities in the system is entered down the left-hand side of the grid and across the top. Each pair of entities defined in the grid is examined to establish whether a direct relationship exists between them. Direct relationships are indicated on the grid by means of a 'X' in the appropriate box. If you are not sure about the nature of a relationship, place a '?' in the box.

	HOTEL	GUEST	ROOM	SUPPLIER	REGION
HOTEL			X	X	X
GUEST			X		
ROOM					
SUPPLIER					X
REGION					

Figure 3.2 Logical Data Structure Matrix

In this example, while at first sight we might think that guest and hotel are related, on further examination we can see that this is an indirect relationship via room.

3.3.4 Convert the Matrix to a Logical Data Structure

The entities and their direct relationships are then represented on the LDS. Entities are depicted by boxes with the singular form of the name of the entity inside.

The entities which are directly related to each other are connected by a straight line. These lines are called 'Access Paths' and may be traversed in either direction. We examine the relationship in both directions looking firstly, in this example, at how one room relates to hotel; in other words, how one particular occurrence of the entity 'room' relates to occurrences of the entity 'hotel'. By occurrence we mean one particular room with its associated attributes such as colour, type (double, etc.), view, etc.

We can see that one room is located in one particular hotel (one-to-one relationship). When we look at the relationship in the other direction, that is, how one hotel relates to room, we know that a particular hotel can have more than one room in it and thus we have to show this on our diagram by using a 'crow's foot' to depict a one-to-many relationship.

The crow's foot notation indicates that for a particular occurrence of the entity without the crow's foot, there may be 0 or more instances of the entity with the crow's foot.

It is more correct to transpose the diagram so that the entity with the single end of the line is above the entity with the crow's feet, giving a hierarchical relation-ship.

In SSADM terminology 'HOTEL' is the Master and 'ROOM' the Detail. Sometimes we may discover that the relationship should be many-to-many.

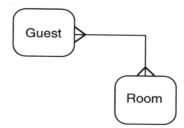

It is possible for one guest to book many rooms over a period of time, and for a particular room to have many guests, again over a period of time. This would give us a many-to-many relationship. This is not allowed in LDM, because such relationships would give rise to ambiguity in the file structure.

In many-to-many relationships there is normally a link between the two entities which will resolve this problem. Usually we can discover a set of data which belongs to this link rather than belonging to either of the entities. If we look at the room:guest relationship more closely, we see that the important link between a particular room and a particular guest is a booking.

The diagram now becomes:

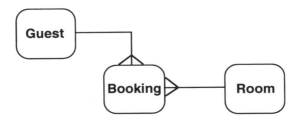

Note that the link entity is always the detail of the other two masters.

In some cases there is not a clearly defined, separate entity as a link and thus we have to design one. For example, a Hotel can use many Suppliers, and each Supplier can serve many Hotels.

The link between the two could well be an order. When an order is placed, it will always be from one hotel to one supplier. The diagram will now become:

3.3.5 Entity Descriptions

During the process of producing the LDS, details of the attributes of each of the entities will evolve. In order to keep a record of these attributes an Entity Description is produced (see Appendix 4).

The description shows all the attributes, including those which will take key values, that is, a field or fields used to define uniquely a single occurrence of a record. The details of format and length of the attributes will not necessarily be entered at this stage but will be added during Stage 6.

3.3.6 Exclusive Relationships

In an LDS it is possible for a detail to be related to more than one master. For example, in our case study, most hotels are organised on a regional basis but 3 report directly to central headquarters. We therefore know that a hotel may be related either to a region or to HQ but not to both. In order to depict this relationship more clearly we use arcs on each of the relationship lines.

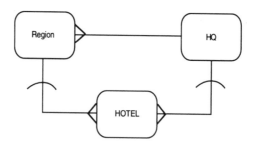

If a master has more than one detail associated with it and only one of the details is possible the arcs are turned round to give the following diagram.

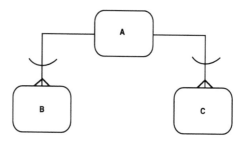

3.3.7 Recursive Relationships

Occasionally it may be that an entity is related to itself. This is called recursion, or involution, and is shown by a 'pig's ear'.

This tells us that a particular employee may supervise, for example, 0, 1 or many other employees, but each employee is only supervised by one other employee. The optionality allows us to have the top person in the company unsupervised.

3.3.8 Rationalise the Structure

Having produced a fairly detailed LDS we now need to rationalise any redundant access paths. Some relationships may be unnecessary because they duplicate access paths already in existence. In example 1 , there is no need for a link between (A) and (C) because the route already exists via entity B. It should be noted that some redundant access paths may have to be reinstated in Stage 6, when we consider the physical design, in order to satisfy performance criteria.

Additionally, the link between A and C would need to be retained if it denoted a different type of relationship, as shown in example 2.

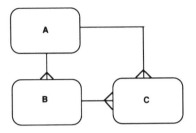

Example 1

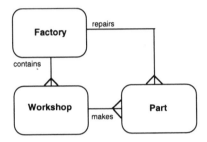

Example 2

3.3.9 Naming Relationships

There is a convention in SSADM of naming relationships between entities; this is recorded in the Entity Description of each entity.

Quite often the production of these descriptive sentences is an aid to the analyst, clarifying the relationship in their mind and acting as an aid to the correct construction of the Logical Data Structure Diagram.

For each relationship there are two relationship descriptions, one which describes the relationship of an occureance of the master entity with the detail entity(ies) and one describing the relationship between an occurrence of the dtail and its master.

The construction of each sentence is governed by a set of key phrases (the italics indicate a choice or completion of a detail)

- each *entity name (1)*

- *may be / must be*

- description or label for the relationship

- *one and only one / one or more*

- *entity name (2)*

Following this convention the following are examples of the named relation-ships for the Hotel System.

- each Booking must be held by one and only one Guest

- each Booking must be linked to one and only one Room Type

- each Occupancy may be linked to zero or more Bar Charge

- each Bar Charge must be the responsibility of one and only one Occupancy

The Logical Data Structure for the Current Hotel System is shown in Figure 3.3

3.4 Data Store/Entity Cross Reference

A Data Store/Entity Cross Reference should be produced from the LDS, the Entity Descriptions and the DFDs. This aids the validation of DFD/LDS dia-grams, ensuring that for all entities on the LDS and their attributes there is a corresponding data store in which they will be held. A Data Store/Entity cross reference for the case study current system is shown in Figure 3.4.

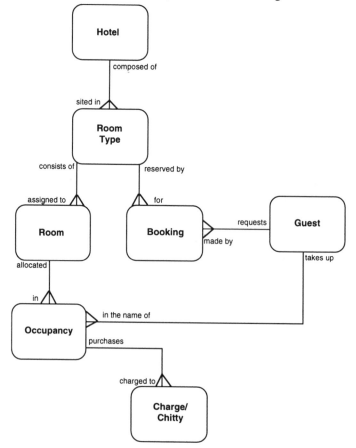

Figure 3.3 : Logical Data Structure of Current Hotel System

Data Store/Entity X - Ref   Page   of

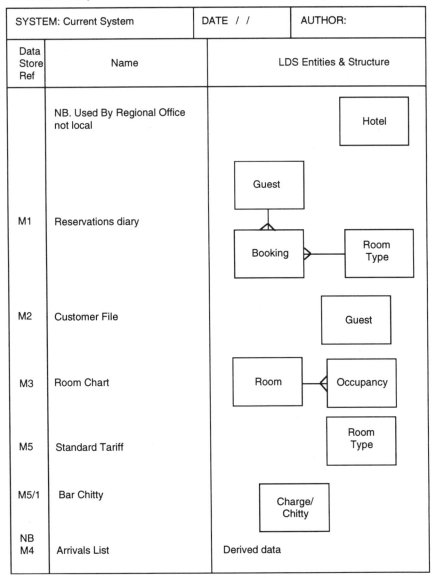

Figure 3.4 LDS/Entity Cross Reference

3.5 Conclusion

This chapter has introduced Logical Data Structures, and the Data Store/Entity Cross Reference.

The work of Stage 1 now requires consolidation through Steps 150 and 160 (Chapter 4) to finalise the Current Environment Structure, enabling these products to move forward into Stage 2.

4 Completion of Stage 1 and Stage 2

4.1 Introduction

This chapter will bring together the final tasks involved in Stage 1. Many of these tasks involve completion of documentation that supports the DFD and LDM. The analyst must then define a logical system by converting the Current Physical Model to a Current Logical Model before moving into Stage 2 and the selection of Business System Options.

A word of warning: Stage 1 can appear both confusing and overwhelming to inexperienced practitioners in view of the variety of techniques employed. The value of some of the techniques may not be immediately obvious, as they may not be picked up again until later in the method. Suffice it to say that in the authors' view it is important to complete all the tasks, however briefly, and wait for all to be revealed in stages 4-6!

4.2 Consolidate Requirement Catalogue (Step 120, 160)

The requirement catalogue was initiated in Step 110 and should have been added to during Step 120 in parallel with the production of the Data Flow Diagrams and the Logical Data Structure (steps 130 and 140).

It is quite feasible that there are a number of people involved in steps 120/130/140 and that all of them have been adding to the RC in an ad hoc manner. In step 160 the RC is examined and duplication removed. Rationalisation of problems/requirements may also be needed. For example, a problem may be 'current billing procedure is too slow' and a requirement may be 'produce bill within two minutes'. These can obviously be combined into one requirement. Once this has been completed the analysts, with the assistance of the users, should allocate priority to each of the requirements.

It should be noted that the RC may also be added to during Stage 2.

4.3 Quality Assurance Reviews

The Quality Assurance Reviews in Version 4 of SSADM have been taken out of the methodology and passed to the Project Management role; it is within that environment that the review methods will be defined.

There are, however, quality criteria defined within the Product Description for each of the SSADM products. These criteria must be studied and applied individually to the products throughout the project and an example of consistency and validation of the LDM product is given in Chapter 3 section 3.4.

4.4 Define the Logical System (Step 150)

This is achieved by Conversion of the Current Physical System DFDs to DFDs of the Current Logical System.

In this procedure, the DFDs from Step 130 are analysed in order to produce a set of DFDs of the current system which show only the logically required processes and data. All the physical limitations which may result from the tools available, historical division of labour, in-built delays, etc., are removed. Having reduced the current system to its essential components, it is possible, at a later stage, to build up a picture of the required system in its logical form, by adding the features identified in the problems/requirements list. By producing logical DFDs we can identify the essence of the current system and at the same time avoid the danger of the analyst being 'blinkered' by the quirks/physical constraints of the current system.

The logical DFDs for the case study can be found Appendix 2.

4.5 Steps in Converting the Physical DFDs to Logical DFDs

4.5.1 Rationalisation of Data Stores

• Remove data stores only needed in the current physical system to handle delays in processing (e.g. an in-tray holding customer enquiries until the receptionist has time to deal with them). Some delay may be logically unavoidable (e.g. if an individual quotation has to be prepared before an enquiry can be processed). In this case the data stores must remain.

• Edit the names of the data stores to remove any physical element, e.g. 'reservations diary' becomes 'reservations'.

• Convert the reference numbers from M (Manual) to D (Data) as the data stores should no longer be regarded as physical files.

• Combine data stores holding the same or similar data, for example in two different physical forms. Look for apparently different data stores using the same key field or attribute, e.g. customer number, to pick out a particular record.

• Split/add/remove data stores. Check that Logical Data Stores correspond to one entity or group of related entities on the LDS. (An entity should appear in only one data store.) The Data Store/Entity Cross Reference (started in Stage 1) should be completed at this stage to record this matching process.

4.5.2 Rationalise the Processes

• Remove the location information from the process boxes.

• Remove processes which merely rearrange data (e.g. sorts) and which are only necessary because of the way in which the data is currently held.

• Remove any physical aspects of the process, e.g.'ink in confirmed booking' changes to 'confirm booking'.

• Combine related processes which are only separate because of historical or political reasons or owing to geographical separation of individuals, departments, etc.

- Combine duplicated processes.
- Split up over-complex processes into two or more simpler processes.
- Regroup 'bottom level' processes. Processes on the low level DFDs should be regrouped by function rather than by location. A process/data store matrix can be used to show those processes that access the same data stores. These processes may then be grouped, linking those which support day-to-day activities, those which maintain reference information and those which are periodic functions. Processes with the same trigger are likely to be grouped together. Having regrouped the lower level DFDs, the top level logical DFD will then need to be redrawn.

4.5.3 Rationalise Data Flows

- Edit the names of data flows to remove any reference to physical documents, e.g. 'registration form' becomes 'registration detail'.
- Identify flows of the same or similar data (although each may be previously labelled as a different document) and give each the same name.

4.5.4 Further Checks

- Add any further problems identified during 'logicalisation' to the RC.

- Verify the logical DFDs against the LDS and amend either or both if necessary.

- Check that all the changes between the physical and logical DFDs can be justified. Amend any elementary function descriptions (process descriptions) as necessary.

4.6 Assembling Results

Finally in Step 160 the results must be assembled and the integrity of all the products checked.

The completeness and consistency of the Current Services Description, which consists of the products listed below,

> Context Diagram
> Current Environment Logical DFD
> Logical Data Model
> Logical Data Store/Entity Cross Reference
> Requirements Catalogue
> User Catalogue

are checked and any amendments made. The Requirements Catalogue is reviewed and consolidated, checking with the relevant users for correctness. Again we would stress that users are consulted at all the stages about all of the products!

The Current Services Description, Requirements Catalogue and User Catalogue are now ready to be utilised in the next stage of the project, Business Systems Options (Stage 2).

4.7 Stage 2 - Business System Options

Business System Options (Steps and Products shown in Figure 4.1) are outline proposals which describe 'what the system should do' rather than 'how it will do it'. The set of options should be designed to give the user the opportunity to decide what approach should be taken to solve the particular problems of this part of his business. It is normal for the analyst to produce a number of options for discussion with the user. The result of these discussions may be that any one of the proposed options is chosen, none is chosen (and the analyst is sacked!), or a hybrid of features from different options is decided upon. This choice then enables the analyst to proceed with the detailed logical design of the proposed system.

Business system options should show the user a number of ways in which the requirements may be satisfied, excluding consideration of hardware and software constraints. Typical options could include central storage versus local storage of data (e.g. a central reservations system or a separated reservation system for each hotel), inclusion versus exclusion of certain functions in the system (e.g. bar receipts automatically recorded or excluded from the system).

4.8 Development of the BSO Set

The BSO should include a top level DFD and a brief description of each option, together with a rough estimate of how much each of the options will cost to implement, along with their respective benefits. It should also detail how the proposed system will be implemented and list any implications for the business ('impact analysis'). It is inevitable that some thought must be given to hardware in order to estimate the cost involved, but this should be at a superficial level, e.g. a mainframe, a network of 12 personal computers, etc.

The Business System Options are best initiated by having a brainstorming session. The documentation which will provide the background material for this session should be

- Requirements Catalogue
- Top level Logical Dataflow Diagram
- Logical Data Structure

The latter two products are only produced if appropriate and the aim should be to define 3 to 4 different options.

Another technique to get started is to produce a BSO that fulfils the minimum requirements and one that incorporates all requirements and many features

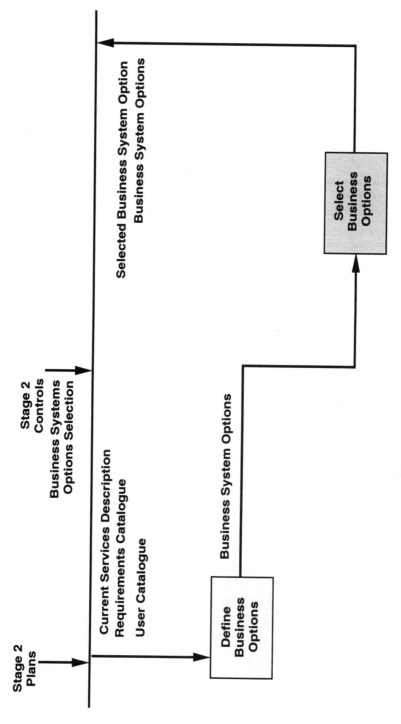

Figure 4.1 Steps in Stage 2

(sometimes called 'all singing, all dancing'). These two will delineate the range and the intermediate skeleton option(s) can then be developed, perhaps using brainstorming as before.

If a feasibility study has not been carried out, a larger number of skeleton BSOs may be needed, possibly as many as 6. These BSOs should cover as many alternative approaches as possible, but each BSO should fall within the constraints of

- the minimum requirements that must be met
- the boundary and scope of the system as defined in the PID and refined in the Current System Investigation
- User and Task identification

The developers should then discuss the skeleton options informally with the users so that options that are totally unsuitable are rejected. The remaining options (two/three) are subjected to an outline cost/benefit and impact analysis and are then presented at a formal Quality Assurance Review Selection meeting.

On the initial BSOs there may be combinations of clerical, computer and clerical/computer processes. On the final BSOs from which the user will make his selection, there should only be computer processes, according to SSADM. However, for completeness and to show clearly the boundary of the computer system it may be desirable to show major clerical processes. It is hoped that one BSO will be chosen, but sometimes, as stated above, a number of features from different BSOs are preferred. If this is the case the details should be noted and used as the basis for the logical design of the proposed system.

A sample BSO for the case study can be found in Appendix 3, while the Level 1 Data flow diagram for this option is shown in Figure 4.2.

4.9 Conclusion

Once the user has selected his preferred option, the analyst can begin to specify the requirements of the new system in more detail, using the logical DFDs and LDS of the current system, together with the Requirements Catalogue, User Catalogue and DFD for the chosen option as a starting point.

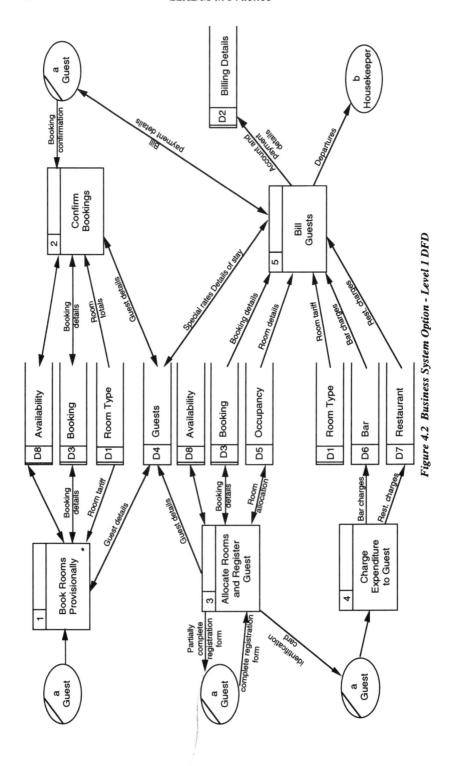

Figure 4.2 Business System Option - Level 1 DFD

5 Stage 3 - Requirements Specification

5.1 Introduction

In the previous chapter, we looked at Stages 1 and 2 in which the current system was analysed into its logical components and the user selected the broad approach to be adopted for the new system. Having defined what the new system is intended to achieve in outline, we can now move into Stage 3 and start to specify the requirements in more detail. The steps and products of Stage 3 are shown in Figure 5.1.

5.2 Defining Required System Processing

Step 310 produces documentation that updates the RC to reflect the required system, develops an outline description in the form of system dataflows and defines the user roles in the required system. This step will progress in parallel with Step 320 which develops the Data Model in a similar way. The following tasks are carried out and documentation is amended or created to support the development of the required system model.

5.2.1 Requirements Catalogue

The RC is reviewed to identify any entries that are no longer part of the 'selected' required system. These entries should be examined and the reasons for their exclusion should be noted in the catalogue.

5.2.2 DFDs

The required system DFDs will need to incorporate solutions or processes identified in the RC and the BSO. They should also be checked against the current logical DFDs to ensure that all the essential facilities have been included in the new system. The DFDs for the Case Study new system are shown in Appendix 4.

5.2.3 Elementary Process Descriptions

Updated or new Elementary Process Descriptions should be created for complex processes on the bottom level DFDs. See Appendix 4.

5.2.4 Input/Output Descriptions

Any new flows crossing the system boundary will require an Input/Output description and existing flows should be checked for correctness. These are

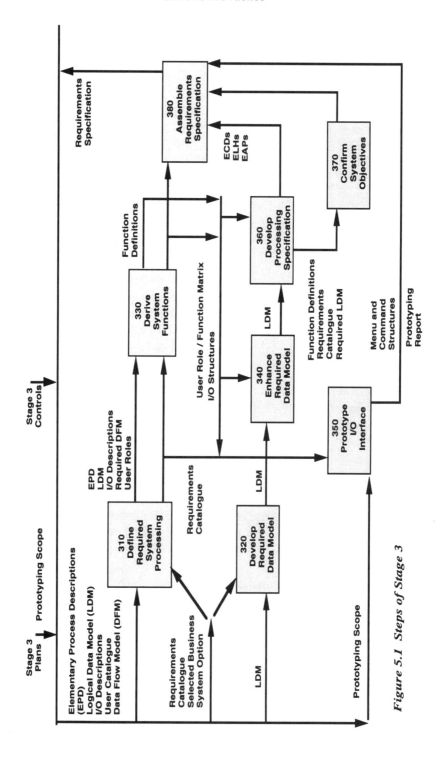

Figure 5.1 Steps of Stage 3

identified from the content of the dataflows. (See Appendix 4). If new External Entities have been identified ensure that a description of that entity is completed.

5.2.5 Data Stores

Each Data Store should be checked; each should consist of one or more entities from the LDS. Flows to and from Data Stores must be examined for consistency with the attributes of the entities.

5.2.6 User Roles

During the initial stages of investigation of the current environment a User Catalogue was compiled; this consisted of the name of a system user (e.g. employee name), their job title and the tasks or activities that they perform. This catalogue is now examined in order to allocate a set of 'User Roles' for the system.

This allocation is done by looking for closely related tasks; for example, in the Hotel System all the tasks related to making a booking could be grouped together into a user role called 'Reservations'.

The tasks do not need to be carried out at the same time, nor by the same individual; in fact quite often closely related sets of tasks are carried out by many different individuals in an organisation. What is important to the analyst is the close relationship of those tasks, and the concept of user role is a convenient way to package those activities. This leads to a clearer understanding of what data is required, where, when and by whom. In addition the packaging of linked activities assists in decisions related to the structure of processes in the system.

Taking the Job Titles and activities from the User Catalogue, a list of User Roles is compiled with the following details

User Role Name (Identifier)

Job Details (Job Titles of those people currently involved in the activity, activities and a brief description of these activities)

If during compilation it is found that more than three Job Titles are covered by one User Role, further investigation should be carried out to clarify or amend the situation, as this could indicate a duplication of tasks.

Examples of both the User Catalogue and User Roles can be found in Appendix 4.

User roles are subsequently used for Dialogue Design and Functional Definition.

5.3 Development of Required Data Model

In Step 320 the Logical Data Model must be updated to reflect the desired processing of the required system.

A new LDM is produced from the Current Environment LDS amended to include only the aspects required by the selected BSO. Each entity description must at this point have all its attributes defined and the RC is updated to reference any new requirements which have emerged during this step.

The Elementary Process Descriptions are checked to ensure that they can be supported by this amended Data Model.

5.4 Derive System Functions (Step 330)

The products of this step are new, rather than amended versions of existing products, and demand much cross-referencing, consultation with users and discussion between project team members. The products are Function Definitions, Input/Output Structures and a User Role/Function Matrix.

5.4.1 What is a function ?

A function is a set of linked system processes that are triggered by the same event and that are therefore carried out at the same time. A function consists of the input, the processes (update and enquiry) required to respond to that input, and the output produced by those processes (see figure 5.2). These functions will become part of the program specification later in the development procedure.

5.4.2 Function Types

Functions can be categorised in three ways:

- Enquiry or update (note that an update function may also include enquiries)

- On-line and off-line - a function can include both types of processing

- Method of initiation, e.g. by the action of a user of the system, a time clock, an error, etc.

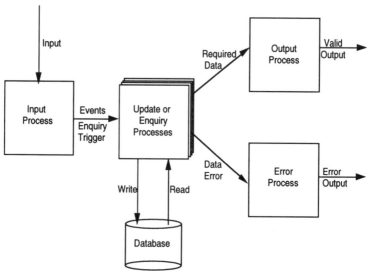

Figure 5.2 Stage 3 Components of a Function

5.4.3 Where to Find Functions

Update functions will be found as processes, a process or a group of processes on the bottom level DFDs. Some enquiry functions may also be found there, however in general the enquiry functions will be found in the RC where they have been identified by the user as a requirement.

5.4.4 Update Functions

The initial identification derives from the Required System DFDs in consultation with the Users, but may be added to later as new events are identified.

Deciding which of the processes can be grouped together into functions can be difficult, but the questions that one should ask are reviewed below:

Examine the processes and ask the following questions in order of priority:

(a) When and how often will a process happen? This may be daily, weekly, on-demand, etc. Group together processes that occur at the same time interval, bearing in mind that although two processes are performed monthly, for example, they may not occur on the same date and thus may need to be kept separate.

(b) Is there a group of processes which act on the same data, e.g. create and amend guest records?

If so, group these together.

(c) Is there a group of processes performing the same function on different sets of data, e.g. archiving guest details and archiving reservation history? If so, group these processes together.

(d) Does a group of processes belong to the same user area, e.g. Accounts? Group these together only if there is no conflict with (a) to (c) above.

5.4.5 Defining Enquiry Functions

Using the Requirements Catalogue, Required System DFD and direct consultation with the system users, some of the previous questions can be applied to the findings to help make the grouping decisions. For example, if an enquiry into the status of a guest is always carried out before the enquiry into availability for a booking, the two enquiries could be grouped together, satisfying (d) in the list of questions.

An example of Function Definition for the hotel system is shown in Figure 5.3 and Appendix 4.

Function Definition	Function Name : *Generate Booking*	ID : *1*

User Roles : *Reservation Clerk*

Function Description :
On receipt of a booking enquiry, dates, room type and number of guests are checked in Room Availability, if available a booking offer is made. If the booking offer is accepted guest and booking details are recorded as a provisional or confirmed booking. On receipt of confirmation the confirm indicator is set. If changes to the booking are requested, availability is checked as for enquiry. If the changes are viable the booking details are changed and the confirmed indicator set. If not, the booking is cancelled and a letter sent to the guest. Guest details can be amended during the booking procedure.

Error Handling :

DFD Processes :
1.1,1.2,1.4,2.1,2.2,2.3,2.4,2.5

Events (Frequency) :
Booking Enquiry, New Provisional Booking, New Confirmed Booking, Confirmed Booking, Booking Change, Booking Cancelled, Amend Guest Details

I/O Descriptions :
Booking Enquiry, Booking Offer, Booking Confirmation, Booking Changes, Notification, Cancellation, Amendment of Guest Details

I/O Structures :
Booking Enquiry, Provisional Booking, Confirmed Booking, Changed Booking

Requirements Catalogue Refs :

Volumes :

Related Functions :
Registration, Allocation, Raise Guest Bills, Maintenence

Enquiries (Frequency)

Common Processing :

Figure 5.3 Function Definition - Booking

5.4.6 Input/Output Structures

This is the specification for the User Interface. Input/Output Structures for Update functions find their basis in the Input/Output Descriptions that support the DFD; the Enquiry function interface is specified in consultation with system users. The I/O Structures consist of a Structure Diagram and a Structure Description - see section 5.5 below.

5.5 Structure Diagrams

SSADM uses a Jackson-style notation,with specific SSADM extensions, for these structure diagrams. The technique of construction of structure diagrams is discussed here in some depth because it is an important technique that the analyst needs to use as a transferable skill throughout the remaining areas of the project. This style of diagram will be required for:

- Function Definition

- Dialogue Design

- Entity/Event Modelling

- Logical Database Process Design

There are notational and syntactic differences that are product specific, which will be explained within each product reference. However, the following sections cover the basic composition, notation and syntax of all structure diagrams.

5.5.1 The Nodes

Structure diagrams consist of a hierarchy of nodes. The Structure Diagram is decomposed top-down; the 'root' node at the top of the structure represents the subject. For an I/O Structure it would be the function name; in an Entity Life History, the entity name, etc.

The next level defines the 'root' node and each node at this level may be further defined at a lower level. An elementary node is one which has no further decomposition. A node may represent any of the following:

Sequence - the node represents one of a number of components occurring in a definite order (left to right).

Selection - the node represents one of a number of components, from which one and only one may be selected at any one time.

Iteration - the node represents a component that may occur a number of times (zero, one or many).

Parallelism - occurs only in an Entity Life History (ELH) and will be explained in Chapter 7.

Operations - the node represents an activity. Operations are only used in structure diagrams for Entity/Event modelling, Dialogue Design and Logical Database Process design.

5.5.2 Notation

A node is represented by a box; the hierarchy of levels is shown by connecting lines and the types of nodes outlined above are shown as follows:

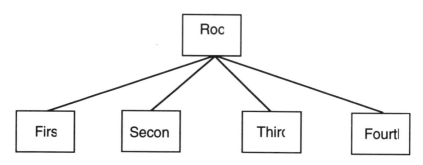

Sequence - Read left to right

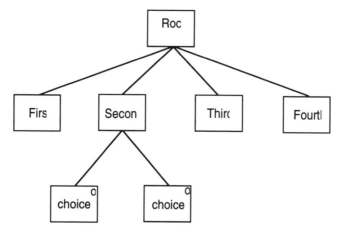

Selection - has a 'o' symbol in each selectable box

Note that the preceding figures have been constructed with diagonal connecting line; this is done to demonstrate this particular method of construction which is the standard recommended in the SSADM manuals. Individuals may prefer alternatives, and provided that the project or organisation has an agreed standard this is quite acceptable. All subsequent diagrams use a straight connection line, as this is the preferred option of the authors for this project.

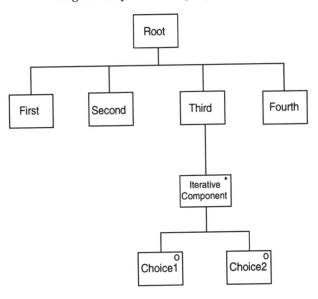

Iteration (consisting of a selection) - If a node in a sequence represents an iteration it must have exactly one box below containing an asterisk symbol '*' to represent the iteration.

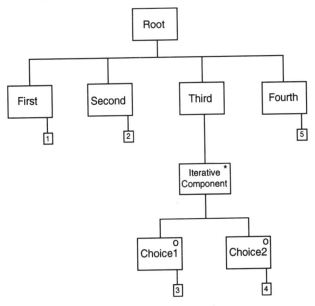

Operations - are denoted by smaller boxes containing a number; these numbers are keys to documented descriptions of the operations.

5.5.3 Syntax Rules

Nodes are represented by boxes and each node must be connected to the next level down by a line. The accepted syntax is that the next level down is drawn lower on the page. To clarify the terminology used in the rules below: a node at the next level down and connected to the one above is termed a 'child' of the higher node. Child nodes with the same parent node are called 'siblings'.

- The Root node should have only one element

- All nodes below root must have exactly one parent

- All sibling nodes must be of the same node type (e.g. selection)

- The node with iteration symbol must be the 'only' child at that level although it may have children of its own

- Selection nodes must have more than one child

- Every node (excepting the root) must have a line connection to a parent

- No links between siblings are allowed (except through parent)

- No crossed lines are permitted

- Parallelism is only permissible in Entity Life Histories (see Chapter 7)

- Every component of parallelism must be part of a sequence (see Chapter 7)

5.5.4 Construction of I/O Structures for On-Line Functions

Once a function has been identified, the analyst must identify all input and output flows for that function. These flows represent the dialogue between the user and the system.

The I/O descriptions from Stage 1 can be used as a starting point and discussion with the user will further identify groups of data items that the user inputs to the system and the responses that the system is expected to make to those inputs. Although some of these data items may appear on the I/O Descriptions if they are input from or output to the system environment, many others will only be represented by data flows, not as yet documented in detail.

When grouping data items

- input and output must not be grouped together

- repeating groups must not be grouped with items outside of the group, i.e. the order lines on an order (repeating) are not grouped with the order number or customer details

- mandatory and optional items are not grouped together, i.e. Customer Details on an order (mandatory) and delivery address (optional)

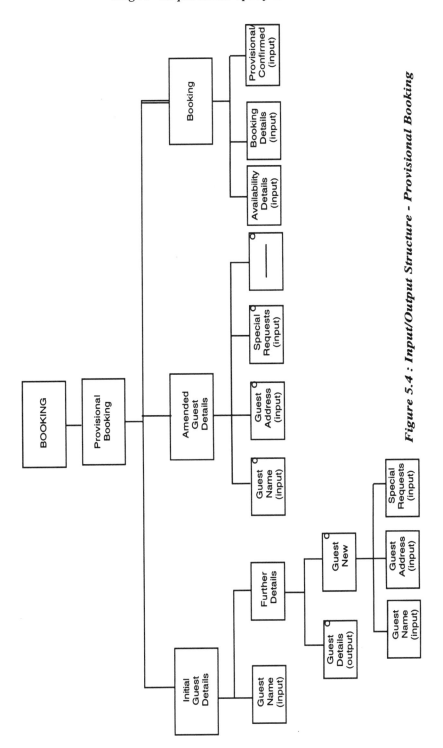

Figure 5.4 : Input/Output Structure - Provisional Booking

Bearing these rules in mind the analyst must identify

• groups of data input by the user

• groups of data items that are the system responses

• the sequencing of those groups of data

The I/O Structure diagram can now be drawn to represent the sequencing of inputs and outputs. See Figure 5.4 for an example.

For example, a function to make a Provisional Booking may look like Figure 5.3.

The Input/Output Structure Description then records each element or node of the diagram and the Input/Output Structure diagram may look like Figure 5.4.

Element	Data Item	Comments
Initial Guest Detail	Guest Name	Mandatory
Further Details	Guest Details	Selection
	New Guest	Selection
	Guest Name	Sequence
	Guest Address	Sequence
	Special Req.	Sequence
Amend Guest	Guest Name	Selection
Details	Guest Address	Selection
	Special Req.	Selection
Booking	Availability Details	Sequence
	Booking Details	Sequence
	Provisional Conf.	Sequence

5.5.5 I/O Structures for Off-Line Functions

As off-line functions do not have to represent iteration between a user and the system because there is no interactive dialogue, each input and output has a separate I/O Structure. In other respects the guidelines for constructing the I/O Structures are the same as for on-line functions.

5.5.6 Further Examples

Further use and construction of the SSADM Structure diagram will be covered in later stages of the system development. A range of Input/Output Structures for the case study are shown in Appendix 4.

5.6 User Role / Function Matrix

Having defined the functions of the Required System a User Role/Function Matrix can now be constructed. This takes information from the User Roles List and cross-references it with the defined functions, thus describing the detail of where each user role fits within the Required System and the commonality of functions to different roles. The matrix is constructed quite simply; taking the System Users on one axis and the functions on the other, the matrix is completed as shown in Figure 5.5.

Functions / Roles	Booking	Allocation	Registration	Acounting	Maintenance
Reservations	*				
Reception		*	*	*	
Local Management					*
Regional Management					*
Bar Cashier				*	
Restaurant Cashier				*	

Figure 5.5 User Role / Function Matrix from Hotel System

5.7 Specification Prototypes (Step 350)

Specification prototyping may be used to describe critical parts (making use of the User Role/Function Matrix) of the requirements specification in an animated form. Only selected areas are covered, as it would be impractical in most system development to prototype all elements. The purpose of this prototyping is to demonstrate to the users correct understanding of the requirements and to establish any additional requirements concerning the Input/Output interface.

The selection or scope of the prototyping is specified as part of the Project Management function and the prototyping will be used to develop menus and command structures (Chapter 9) for selected user roles. The remainder of the menu and command structures are completed in Stage 5, thus working in close interaction with Step 330 (Derive System Functions).

The use of prototyping has to be very tightly controlled, as it is too easy to fall into the trap of iterating the process too many times. Users can become very enthusiastic when offered an animated demonstration and their demands can become overwhelming, 'That is wonderful, now it would be even better if... '. Although this is the reaction needed, the reader will see that this can be like giving a child free run of a toy shop! It is therefore very important that limits are set to the number of iterations the prototype process will go through. SSADM suggests that the maximum should be three iterations, so that if this is laid down at the start then everyone becomes more focused in their demands.

The other important point that the analyst must ensure the users are aware of is that this is just a prototype, not a working system. The danger otherwise is that user's will see the prototype as part of the system, and they will wonder why they cannot start using it immediately.

Despite the dangers, prototyping is a very good way of enthusing the users, getting them involved and engendering a feeling of ownership of the system.

5.7.1 Prototyping Documentation

There are four documentation products associated with prototyping; these are

- Prototype Pathways - these detail the menus, screens and reports that are to be demonstrated by the prototype, i.e. what elements of the required system are to be prototyped.

- Prototype Demonstration Objective Documents - one for each pathway to document the method and the objectives of the demonstration.

- Prototype Result Logs - one for each pathway to document the result of the prototype demonstration and any actions that need to be taken.

- Menu and Command Structures - these are then referred to at the later stage of Dialogue Design (Chapter 8).

5.8 Conclusion

Chapter 5 has introduced the largest stage of the project, that of specifying the required system. Accuracy and completeness are of extreme importance; in this stage the analyst is producing all the foundations for the more specific design areas in later stages.

We have also introduced the structured diagram, a technique that will now be used throughout the project under different names to represent information diagrammatically. It is therefore an important technique to understand and master.

6 Step 340 - Enhance Required Logical Data Model

6.1 Introduction

Relational data analysis (RDA) and Logical data modelling (LDM) are two different but complementary ways to identify and specify data requirements. LDM works from the top down, taking an overview of the data model and gradually adding more information, while RDA works from the bottom up, starting with arbitrary data groups and forming larger groups that correspond to the entities and relationships of the LDM.

Having specified input and output data items on the I/O Structure Descriptions during Function Definition, these specifications can now be used for Relational Data Analysis. The results of this analysis are compared with the existing LDM to highlight any structural differences, which need to be resolved using judgment based on knowledge of present and future processing requirements. It should be noted that often the optimal structure is not achieved until Entity Life History Analysis is complete (see Chapter 7).

6.2 Relational Data Analysis (RDA)

Relational Data Analysis (RDA) is complementary to LDM. The LDM is derived, in part, from an examination of the data shown on the DFDs. It concentrates on groups of data and on the relationships between them, rather than on the detailed contents of each data group. RDA, on the other hand, is derived from the Function Definitions and focuses on the data items within each data group. RDA may also be referred to as Third Normal Form Analysis (TNF), so called because it is carried out in three steps.

For RDA the analyst must select the system functions to be used as source. It would more often than not be impractical to normalise all the inputs and outputs of a system. This selection will be based on the experience of a senior analyst but should normally encompass the most critical system functions.

Having made the selection RDA is performed on the input/output data items, creating a set of normalised relations for each chosen function. These relations are then converted into an LDM sub-model. This sub-model is compared to the relevant section of the system LDM; differences are resolved by reference to the processing requirements and to users. The LDM is then updated using the new entities and relationships.

Normalisation is a powerful technique for analysing and representing data at the logical level, regardless of how the data is to be stored. As previously mentioned, the process is carried out in three steps, at the end of which a set of normalised relations is produced. Each relation or data group contains related data items which are dependent on a particular key.

61

6.2.1 Keys

In order to be able to explain RDA a number of terms have to be defined:

• Key - a key is a data item used to identify a particular occurrence of an entity. If the key is not unique a number of occurrences may be selected.

• Primary key - a primary key is a key consisting of a data item or group of data items, uniquely identifying an occurrence of an entity.

• Secondary key - a secondary key does not uniquely identify an occurrence of an entity but may be used to select a number of occurrences which match a particular (secondary key) value.

• Compound key - this is a primary key which is composed of more than one data item. The data items are always used together to identify uniquely a particular occurrence of the entity. Additionally, each data item of the compound key is normally itself a key of another data group, e.g. the key for booking is made up of room type and guest name, each of which is the key of another group.

Element	Data Item	Comments
Order References	Order Reference	
	Date	
Customer Details	Customer Name	
	Customer Address	
Order Lines	Wine_reference	Iterative
	Description	
	Quantity	
	Price/Case	
	Line Total	Derived
Final Details	Order Total	Derived

Figure 6.1: Input/Output Structure Description - Production of Delivery Note

• Composite key - this is created when the primary key needs further qualification to ensure uniqueness. It is a key which consists of more than one data item, i.e. the main key item and one or more other data items which will act as further qualifiers. For example, a particular car component has a unique number - say engine number. The engine number is unique in that series of engines but the same set of numbers may be used for another set of engines. Thus we would need both the engine number and the engine type (acting as the qualifier) to identify the record uniquely. Unlike a compound key, only the qualifying data items of a composite key may themselves be the key of another data group.

- Foreign key - A foreign key is a non-key data item within one RDA relation which also occurs as a key in another relation. It is used to maintain a link between two relations.

6.3 Normalisation of Data - First Normal Form

The source input/output having been selected, we then choose a key (see 6.2.1) which will uniquely identify a particular (occurrence of the) function. Remember that a key can consist of more than one data item.

The listing of Unnormalised data items, is taken from the I/O Structure Description (for details of these structures see Chapter 5) shown in Figure 6.1.

<u>Order reference</u>
Date
Customer Name
Customer Address
  Wine-reference
  Description
  Quantity
  Price/Case
  Line_total
Order_Total

Order_reference is underlined to show that it has been chosen as the primary key for this data group or relation. The indented data items are a repeating group (iterative data).

In order to convert the data into *First Normal Form (FNF)*, any repeating groups of data itemsare extracted. In the sample delivery note there may be more than one line of wine details on each order. Thus the data items which pertain to each line of the order are treated as a so-called repeating group within a particular order. The repeating group of data items is removed to form a new relation or data group. A key must be chosen which will uniquely identify an occurrence of this new group. The data item wine-reference is chosen as the key for the new data group and other appropriate data items are written underneath. The key of the original relation order_reference is added to the new relationship, thereby forming a compound key with wine-reference which will enable the wine details of a particular order to be extracted. This data group is now in first normal form, i.e. the data group does not contain any repeating groups. The remaining data items in the original relation, together with their key, are now also in first normal form.

FNF

Order_reference
Date
Customer_Name
Customer_Address
Order_total

Order_reference
Wine-reference
Description
Quantity
Price/case
Line_Total

More than one repeating group may be identified at first normal form and, sometimes, there may be a repeating group inside a repeating group. In this case the internal or 'nested' repeating group is extracted to form a separate relation. This relation will have a compound key composed of the compound key of the original repeating group, together with its own key item.

It is sometimes useful to think of repeating groups as being held within sets of brackets. Two examples are shown below. For each level of parenthesis, there must be an additional key in order to extract the information. In example 1, there is a repeating group within a repeating group and thus the innermost relation needs a compound key consisting of three items to extract data.

Example 1

(Region, address (Hotel, address (Room No, room type)))
becomes
<u>Region</u>
address

<u>Region</u>
<u>Hotel</u>
address

<u>Region</u>
<u>Hotel</u>
<u>Room_No</u>
Room_type

Example 2

(Bill Reference, bill total(Wine reference, wine total) (Dinner reference, dinner total))
becomes

<u>BillReference</u>
bill_total

<u>BillReference</u>
<u>WineReference</u>
wine_total

<u>BillReference</u>
<u>DinnerReference</u>
dinner_total

6.4 Second Normal Form Analysis

In *Second Normal Form analysis* we look only at relations which have a compound key and extract any data items which are dependent on only part of the key.

Order reference/Wine reference form a compound key and on examination, it can be deduced that the data items 'description' and 'price/case' are only related to wine reference. In other words they do not change if order reference alters. These data items, together with their key wine reference, are extracted to form a new relation.

FNF	SNF
<u>Order-reference</u>	>
Date	> Stays the
Customer_Name	>
Customer_Address	> same
Order_Total	>
<u>Order-reference</u>	<u>Order-reference</u>
<u>Wine-reference</u>	<u>Wine-reference</u>
Description	Quantity
Quantity	Line_Total
Price/case	
Line_Total	<u>Wine-reference</u>
	Description
	Price/case

At this point we have 3 relations or data groups, all in second normal form, i.e. all partial key dependencies have been resolved.

6.5 Third Normal Form Analysis

In *Third Normal Form analysis* the objective now is to look at the data items in
each relation in order to decide whether or not they are directly dependent on
each other rather than on the designated key. In the example, a particular
customer name will lead to a particular address. Address is more dependent on
customer name than on order reference, so these two items are removed to form a
new relation. The key of the new relation (customer name) is also retained within
the original relation and marked with a '*' to indicate that it is a foreign key. This
is the data item which forms the link between the two relations.

SNF	TNF
Order-reference	Order-reference
Date	Date
Customer Name	Customer Name *
Customer Address	Order_total
Order_Total	
Order -reference	Order-reference
Wine-reference	Wine-reference
Quantity	Quantity
Line_total	Line_total
Wine-reference	Wine-reference
Description	Description
Price/case	Price/case
	Customer Name
	Customer Address

The data groups are now in third normal form, i.e. all the items within a relation
are dependent on its key.

Fourth and fifth steps may also be included within normalisation; for further
information, see *Principles and Practice of Database Systems* by S.M. Deen
(Macmillan 1985).

6.6 Validation after Completion of Normalisation

The relations which have been produced should be validated to check each of the
following:

- each key value will select only one value for each data item that is dependent
  on it

- all data items are directly dependent on the key and nothing but the key. In
  some cases, an additional data item may have to be added to the key to
  ensure uniqueness (see 6.2.1)

6.7 Rationalisation

It is usually the case that, after carrying out normalisation on a set of functions, a number of relations containing similar data items are identified, or more than one relation is found which describes the same set of data. All relations must therefore be examined to see if there is any redundancy. This is achieved by the process of 'optimisation', i.e.

- merging relations with identical keys.

- re-examining keys to see whether different keys relate to the same group of data. There are a number of potential pitfalls to be aware of when carrying out redundancy checks such as:

- keys or data items which may look the same but are not actually the same. For example this often occurs if 'date' is used as the name of a data item. We need to check whether a date which may occur in several data groups actually refers to the same information in each case, e.g. 'date' may refer to 'date of birth' in one case and 'leaving date' in another case. In this instance, although the item appears to be the same at first sight, the two items cannot be merged.

- keys which may look different may actually be the same. This can occur when RDA is carried out by a number of different people. One team may label a data item 'customer no' while another may call it 'account no'. Are they actually the same? Do they refer to the same data? If so, the items can be merged into one data group.

- loss of 'real world' significance; for example, there may be two groups of data, one of which looks like a subset of the other. For example,

GUEST	**BLACK LIST**
Guest Name	Guest Name
Address	Amount outstanding
Tel. no	

On examination, it may be thought that, as they both refer to 'guest' information and have the same key, the two relations can be merged. However, if 'amount outstanding' is merely added to the 'guest' relation, all reference to the guest as a bad payer will disappear once the amount has reduced to 0. In this case therefore, if the structures are merged, a field of 'credit status' may need to be created.

- key only relations (i.e. relations which consist only of a key and contain no other data items). In general, we would expect many key-only relations to be removed during rationalisation. If any such relations persist, they need to be examined to see whether they are really needed or whether they can be discarded. In some cases they may form the only link between two or more relations and therefore should be retained.

- derived data: In carrying out analysis, data items which can be derived from other data within the system should be removed, either during the normalisation stages or at the rationalisation stage. In the delivery note example, the data items 'line-total' and 'order-total' can be calculated from other data and may therefore be removed from the entity descriptions.

On completion of rationalisation, all the resulting relations should be validated again to ensure that they still pass the normalisation tests (see 6.6). If not, they may need to be normalised once more.

Having completed this normalisation of the data the next stage is to merge the LDM for the required system with the optimised RDA relations.

6.8 Conversion of Normalised Relations to an LDM Type Structure

As a first step the normalised relations are converted to a data structure (or number of sub structures) using the following rules:

• Each of the normalised relations becomes an entity on the new LDS. Use system knowledge to name each entity.

• If a relation has a compound key it becomes the detail of other relations on the diagram which have an item of the compound key as their primary key. If any item of the compound key does not occur as a key of a separate master data group, new data group(s) must be created which will be master(s) of the relation with the compound key. Each new data group should contain the relevant data item as its key field.

It is possible for a compound key to consist of more than two components. This can happen when, in the original data used in RDA, there is a repeating group within another repeating group - see the example below. In this event, the resultant LDS will reflect this 'nesting' as shown in Figure 6.2.

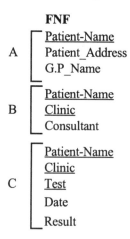

FNF

A
    Patient-Name
    Patient_Address
    G.P_Name

B
    Patient-Name
    Clinic
    Consultant

C
    Patient-Name
    Clinic
    Test
    Date
    Result

• Any relations containing a foreign key should become the detail of the master data group which has the foreign key data item as its key. Referring back to the

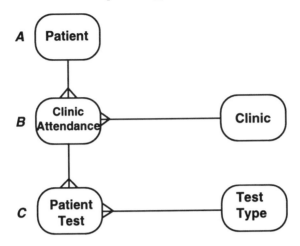

Figure 6.2: Example LDS Segment for Nested Repeating Group

Order example used earlier in the chapter (page there is a foreign key of Customer Name; this would manifest itself, following the above instructions, in the LDS section shown below.

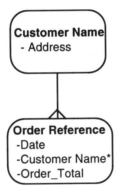

6.9 Merging the Required System LDS with the LDS Sub-Model

The next stage is to combine the LDS for the required system produced in Stage 2 with the LDM created from the optimised RDA relations. Either structure may contain components not found on the other.

Combining the two structures cannot be done by a strict set of rules; however, a set of guidelines is provided. It is important to remember that at this stage any anomalies in the two structures may need to be discussed with the user to clarify the detailed processing requirements.

- Draw the entities and relationships which are the same in both structures.

- Compare data groups from the LDM and the RDA that have multiple masters. Any differences may be due to errors in either structure which need to be resolved.

- Match all remaining data groups across the two structures, either resolving any errors, or evaluating the need for the additional RDA data groups against the processing that will be needed within the system.

- Compare the access paths between the two structures and resolve any differences according to the processing requirements.

- Add details of the additional data groups to the entity descriptions.

6.10 Conclusion

Logical Data Modelling in the earlier stages of development took a 'top-down' view of the data. The LDM Sub-model produced in Stage 3 using Relational Data Analysis builds from a 'bottom-up' view. By merging these two opposite views a level of optimisation is achieved to move into the Data Design phase of the development.

7 Stage 3 : Develop Processing Specification

7.1 Introduction

Step 360 defines the detailed update and enquiry processing that has, thus far, only been outlined in the DFD and Function Definitions. Another major modelling technique is used to enable the analyst to acquire a more detailed understanding of the system. Entity-event modelling leads to further explorations of how the system works and completes the Logical Data Model, providing a specification of database update processing via the effect correspondence technique.

7.2 Entity-event Modelling

Information from the Function Definitions and Enhanced Logical Data Model and other products, (RC, DFD) will be used in Entity-event modelling.

Although the Function Definitions provide the base information for identifying events, new events may be identified during this step, thereby necessitating amendments to or the creation of new Function Definitions.

7.3 Entity Life Histories

Entity Life History Analysis (ELH) is a very important technique in SSADM. It provides a cross-check between the LDS and DFDs of the required system.

In creating the LDS, the entities within the system about which we store data were identified. The purpose of an ELH is to record diagrammatically all of the events which affect the data concerning that entity and identify the order in which they will occur. Any entity must be created within the system. It may be amended several times and it will probably be deleted. ELHs will therefore also highlight any processes, used to change data in the system, which have been omitted from the DFDs.

It is important to remember that ELHs are primarily a record of the events which affect the data; thus careful thought must be given to the naming of the events. Before embarking on the ELHs themselves, it can be helpful to produce an Entity/Event Matrix. An example of part of the matrix for the hotel system is shown in Figure 7.1 and a complete version is in Appendix 4.
N.B. An event is something that invokes a process.

7.3.1 Entity/Event Matrix

As can be seen from Figure 7.1, the entities are entered along the top of the page and the events which affect the entities are written down the left hand side of the page. The entities entered on to the matrix are identified from the Enhanced LDS of the required system. Generally, events are identified by looking at the Function Definitions where necessary supported by the lowest level DFDs.

For each of the events in the matrix an entry must appear against at least one entity. There may, of course, be more than one entry if the event affects more than one entity. Equally, each entity will probably be affected by several events. There are three types of entry on the matrix:

- I - Insertion of an entity occurrence (record)

- M - Modification or amendment of an occurrence (record)

- D - Deletion of an occurrence/record.

SYSTEM:	DATE / /	AUTHOR:		
	GUEST	BOOKING	OCCUPANCY	
New provisional booking	I M	I		
New confirmed booking	I M	I		
Confirmed booking		M		
Booking charge		M		
Cancel booking	D	D		
Change to guest details	M			
Room allocation			I	
Guest registration	I M			
Guest arrival		I		
Room changes			M	
Guest departs	M	D	D	
No guest booking for 2 years	D			
Decoration arranged			I D	
Non arrival			D	

Figure 7.1 : Partial Entity/Event Matrix for Hotel System

7.3.2 Reviewing the Matrix

After the Entity/Event Matrix has been produced it should be reviewed to check the following:

- All entities are created, i.e. have at least one 'I' entry

- All entities have at least one 'D' (Delete) or it has been verified that they are deleted outside the system.

- The events affect at least one entity

At this stage we may find that some processes are missing from the DFDs. These should now be added to the DFD and Function Definitions.

After review, the matrix is used to produce the ELHs. It should be stressed that use of the matrix is a matter of personal choice. The authors do not themselves find it a helpful technique.

7.4 Producing ELH Diagrams

ELH diagrams are constructed using the Structure Diagram notation described in detail in Chapter 5.

The top box in any ELH contains the name of the entity.

Below the entity another box is drawn to represent each of the events in its life cycle. These events must occur in one of the following ways:

1. Sequence - the events follow each other in sequence
2. Selection - one event or another will occur
3. Iteration - the event is repeated a number of times.

It is important that in the diagram the rules concerning parent/sibling relationships are observed as outlined in Chapter 5.

7.4.1 Producing the ELH

In creating the ELHs for a particular system, it is usual to start with the entities at the lowest level of hierarchy in the LDS, i.e. the entities which are only details and are not masters of lower level entities. Having chosen an initial entity, we now look at the Function Definitions and identify the event(s) which create that entity. If there is more than one possible way of creating a particular entity, then this may be represented by a selection under the overall event responsible for triggering the creation process.

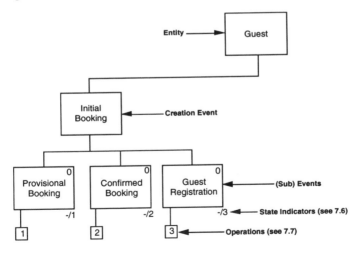

Figure 7.2 The Creation of Guest

It is useful at this point to have the entity descriptions to hand as they contain the attributes of the entity and it may be that all of the data is not entered at the creation point but may be added at a later date; e.g. some of the customer details in the hotel system may only be added after the completion of the registration card on arrival. The events which cause amendments to the entity are now examined and the order of occurrence is determined. In general this is a straight-forward task and the events are entered from left to right across the page. Sometimes, however, there are two or more events which may occur at anytime within the life of the entity. When it is difficult or impossible to know at what precise point an event will occur, we adopt a parallel bar from which to hang all of the relevant events (see 7.4.2).

The deletion events are now added to the ELH. If there is more than one method of deleting the entity then a check must be made to the sequence involving the deletion; e.g. if a booking can be deleted either by the guest's departure or by a non-arrival, the latter cannot be preceded by a series of charges during the amendment phase.

7.4.2 Parallel Bars in the ELH

In chapter 5 the construction of structure diagrams was explained, one notation was left out, that of the parallelism. This notation is unique to the ELH and is used when certain events occur at unpredictable times. In the example below the three events shown under a parallel bar, Update Account, Change Details and Statement Request can happen at any time during the life of an entity occurrrence and in any order; therefore, in this partially constructed ELH parallelism is used to indicate this random event feature.

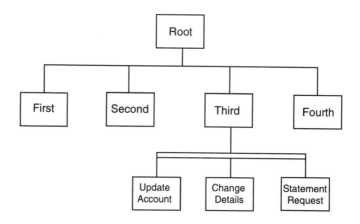

When considering the use of parallelism, great care must be exercised to ensure that the events concerned should and do occur randomly.

7.4.3 Quit and Resume

The constructs of ELH diagrams allow us to use a 'quit and resume' feature in cases when the normal life of an entity may need to be interrupted and resumed at an earlier or later stage.

For example, a guest makes a provisional booking and then telephones later in the day to cancel. Having created a new occurrence of an entity we may wish to delete those details from our system and therefore 'jump' to the deletion event. The convention is to label the 'quit' box with the letter 'Q' and a number (allowing us more than one occurrence of a quit and resume). The box at which we resume is similarly labelled with an 'R' and a matching number. As far as possible, the use of quit and resume should be avoided so that unstructured jumps are minimised.

As the ELHs are created new events will be identified. These should be included in the Function Definitions, either by amending an existing function or creating a new one. Rare events should not be considered at this stage, otherwise the process of producing the ELHs will become too complicated, but if necessary an 'abnormal life' for an entity is produced which deals only with these unusual events.

7.5 Review ELHs

When ELHs have been created for each entity, they should be reviewed and the interdependence between them examined. The review is normally carried out starting at the top of the LDS; that is, those entities which have no master entities are reviewed first. This provides a cross-checking facility, as the ELHs were originally produced from the bottom level entities.

The following should be considered during this review:
- Random events disrupting the sequence of the ELH. Have these events been catered for, e.g. by a quit and resume?
- Effect on a detail when the master is deleted; e.g. should the detail entity also be deleted or transferred to another master? In this case, the same event will need to be entered on the ELH of the detail.
- Effect of deletion on other entities. Again, a deletion event may need to be carried over into other ELHs.

7.6 State Indicators

A State Indicator is a number given to each bottom level event on an ELH diagram. This indicator will also be added to the attributes of an entity and hence the current value of the indicator will become a data item in each occurrence (record) of the entity. Each time the processing for an event is completed the indicator is updated. Consequently, by examining the state indicator we can discover which event affected the entity data most recently.

Additionally, the state indicators on the ELH specify which event(s) must have occurred immediately prior to the current event by defining the previous valid value(s) of the indicator.

Each bottom level leaf of the ELH should have at least one State Indicator attached to it. The numbering should be arbitrary but, as the diagram shows, it is sensible to number sequentially from the left-hand side.

The numbering sequence is in two parts, e.g. 1, 2/3. The number on the right-hand side of the / is the number of that particular event inside the box, whereas the numbers on the left-hand side of the / show which of the events may have preceded this event in the ELH. Thus the 1st box on the left-hand side of the diagram will have a null (-) on the left-hand side of the '/' indicating that no events could have occurred before this one, and similarly the last box on the right-hand side will have a null on the right-hand side of the box to indicate that no further events can occur. The set of valid previous state indicators for an iterating event must include the iteration set value itself.

In the case of parallel bars, only one 'leg' is deemed to affect the main state indicator (see Figure 7.3 which is an example ELH for the Case Study) and the other leg leaves the indicator unchanged. This is depicted by a '*' in the 'set to' value. A subsidiary state indicator (shown in brackets) may be used to control the other less significant leg(s) if required. This subsidiary state indicator will also be a valid setting for the next event after the parallel structure. Some ELHs for the Case Study can be found in Appendix 1.7. The state indicators will be reviewed in Stage 5 - see chapter 9.

7.7 Operations

Operations should now be added to each bottom leaf node on the diagram. An operation node is a box containing a number; this number is a key to a list of operations given either at the base of the ELH or on an attached sheet.

At this point in development the operations will be simple instructions like 'store keys' or 'store other attributes'; the operations will be enhanced in Stage 5. Examples of operations are shown in Figure 7.3.

7.8 Effect Correspondence Diagram

The Effect Correspondence diagram (ECD) is used to validate the ELH in Stage 3 and is subsequently used during the Process Specification activity in Stage 5. One ECD should be constructed for each event identified in ELH analysis and should include each effect caused by the event. The diagram shows the effects that events have on data in the system and how they correspond to each other, thus providing information about the required update access paths used in Stage 5 logical design.

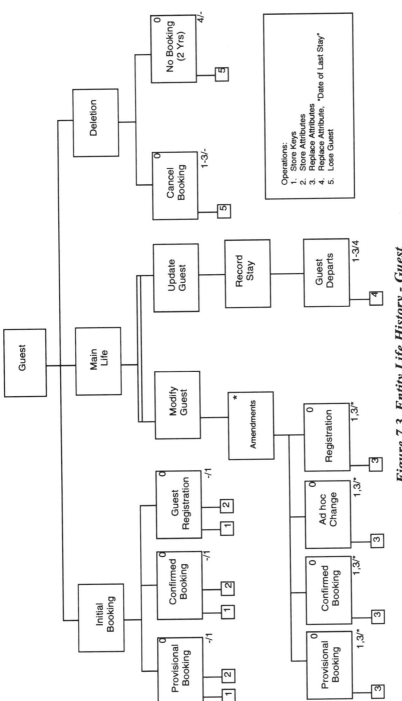

Figure 7.3 Entity Life History - Guest

7.8.1 Construction of the Effect Correspondence Diagram

The SSADM Manual recommends the following seven steps as being the most practical way to develop the diagram, based on practical experience:

1) For each event on the ELHs draw a box representing each entity affected by the event. Look through the ELH set and find all entities that have the same event occurring and include the entity on the ECD.

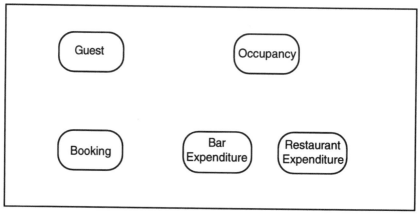

Figure 7.4 : Initial ECD for the event - Guest Departs

2) Draw a separate box for simultaneous effects on the same entity, where each effect is performed in sequence. This is identified on the ELH where an event 'leaf' has a different 'role' in an event for each of the effects.

3) Include optional effects, where there is a selection of one effect only to be performed. This is when an event can effect an entity in two or more mutually exclusive ways.

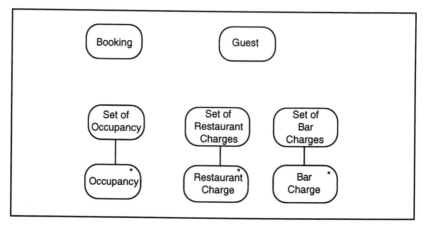

Figure 7.5 : Next level of construction of ECD - Guest Departs

4) Add iterated effects as iterated boxes. This is established by checking the LDS; if a master to detail relationship of 'one to many' is shown then each detail will need updating. The detail node must be notated to show iteration, then a new node representing the set of details is constructed and linked to the iterative node.

5) Add one-to-one correspondence between effects; to do this you need to examine the entities from the LDS that appear in the ECD that have a one-to-one relationship and ask the question

 • If the entity occurrence is updated, is *only* one occurrence of the other entity type updated?

 • If the answer is in the affirmative, then link the nodes on the ECD with an arrow, this arrow shows the direction of correspondence between the two nodes.

6) Merge effects that are iterative. This occurs where an entity is affected in more than one iterative way during an event and where the iterations refer to the same relationship on the LDS. The effects should be merged to show either an iterated selection or a selection of iterations.

7) Add non-updated entities for enquiry purposes. Having dealt with the entities that will be updated by the event, the diagram must now be checked to ensure that all data needed for the event is present. Examine the ECD and ask if all data is represented that is required for output from the event; also is it possible to access all entities on the ECD without using unaffected entities from the LDS? If the answer is no then add the entities in question to the ECD.

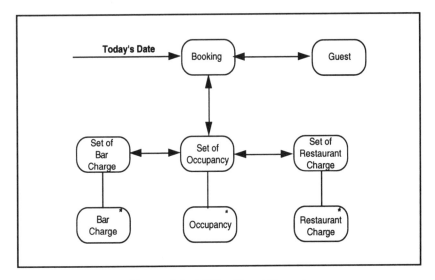

Figure 7.6 : ECD - Guest Departs

The final task is to add event data; this will normally be to show on the diagram the key of the entity that constitutes the entry point to the LDS. The entry point would normally be one of

- primary key (identifier)

- a non-key attribute or attribute that forms part of primary key

- if access is to be to all occurrences of an entity then an unlabelled arrow is used

The event data itself is documented as a list of attributes for the event with repeating groups (if any) represented in some standard way, like indenting or by the use of parenthesis (see Appendix for examples).

7.9 Enquiry Access Path

An Enquiry Access Path defines the entities accessed and the navigation path through the LDM that is required for an enquiry or the enquiry part of an update process.

The Enquiry Access Path (EAP) can be constructed as soon as the LDM is complete; however, there is no hard and fast rule as to when the diagrams are completed and the technique is explained at this point because construction has similarities with the ECD. One reason for carrying out the EAP as early as possible is in order to check the LDS.

7.9.1 Construction of an Enquiry Access Path

The first step is to define the enquiry trigger; this will consist of any information that must be supplied to allow the enquiry to obtain the correct data for output. This will be defined by the input data on the I/O Structure for the enquiry function and would normally contain:

- prime key(s) of any entity to be accessed

- non-key attributes of one or more entities

- the selection criteria for the entity occurrences

Example - Trigger for Booking Enquiry

Guest Name
Date Arrival
Date Depart
Room Type
No. Rooms

The following steps are taken to construct the EAP diagram:

1) Identify the entities that are accessed to obtain or derive the required output. Having identified the entities the LDS should be examined to discover how the enquiry will navigate round the structure. In some cases it may be

necessary to redraw the part of the LDS affected by the enquiry; this is called the 'required view'. This is done by showing access from 'master to detail' as vertical and 'detail to master' as horizontal. This 'required view' can now be enhanced to become the EAP by the addition of arrows showing the way the enquiry will be processed - see Figure 7.8.

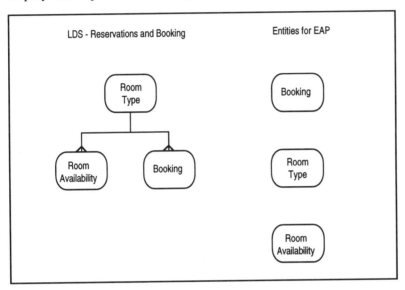

Figure 7.7 : LDS of the 'Required View' for Booking Enquiry

2) Where a single occurrence of one entity corresponds to a single access of a connected entity, put an arrow showing the direction of access - see 'Booking' to 'Room Type' in Figure 7.8.

3) Where more than one occurrence of an entity is required for a single occurrence of a connected entity an iteration must be shown; this is illustrated by an extra box to represent the 'set of' repeated occurrences. This box is then connected to the box representing the repeating occurrence entity, an asterisk being placed in the entity box to indicate iteration. The 'set of' box will also be connected to the single occurrence entity - see 'Room Availability' in Figure 7.8.

4) If the access path is split, offering a choice based on the selection criteria, then a circle is placed in the top right hand corner of each entity box involved in the selection (these will also be drawn at the same level) to indicate 'optionality'.

5) Entry point and input data are now added to the diagram; an arrow is drawn to indicate the entry point for access. The entry point should then be annotated with the essential data required for access. If there is more than one entry point, these should also be identified; if every occurrence of an entity is to be accessed then the arrow is sufficient without any data notation. When data used for access is not the 'prime key' for the entity, this may cause more than

one occurrence to be selected. The diagram should therefore be redrawn with the addition of a 'set of' box as for iteration.

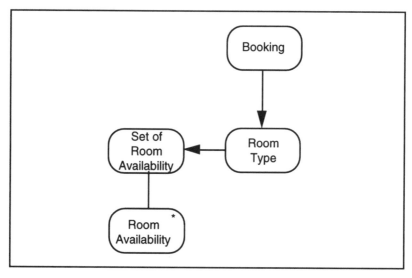

Figure 7.8 : EAP with iteration added

6) The EAP should now be checked to ensure that all data required can be obtained using

   • direct reads to prime key

   • read next detail of a detail from a master

   • read directly master from detail

   and that derived data has all inputs that are required for calculation.

The EAP completed is now passed as part of the function definition to the next stage of process specification. The completed Enquiry Access Path for the booking enquiry is shown in Figure 7.9.

The EAP is initially developed to check the validity of the LDM by checking that the data needed for an enquiry can be obtained via the route through the LDS that is depicted on the EAP. The EAP is then used in the development of Enquiry Process Models.

7.10 Conclusion

Entity/Event Modelling provides a sound basis for later development of the process specifications and logical design. The techniques have been described in this chapter and an effort has been made to provide a step-by-step guide to the Entity Life History and Effect Correspondence Diagram construction. The inexperienced analyst should recognise that in all cases a sound understanding of the system involved is essential for success in applying any of the techniques.

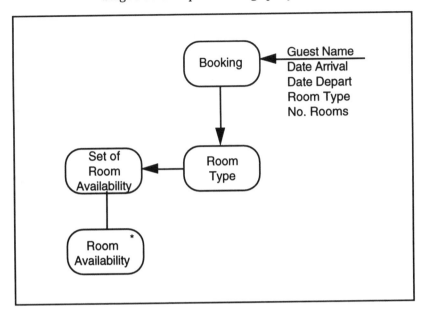

Figure 7.9: EAP for booking enquiry

8 Stage 4 : Selection of Technical Systems Options

8.1 Introduction

Much of the work carried out in Stage 4 can be thought of as relating to the guidelines within project management as much as to SSADM, and thus the methods used to produce, for example, the performance objectives, may differ from project to project. In terms of SSADM there is a need for interaction with project management and other expertise to provide the information required to shape the Technical Systems Options. The main aim of this stage is to provide a firm basis for development of the system.

During Stage 3 of SSADM the analyst is trying to produce a logical specification for the system which will satisfy the user's requirements. In Stage 4 a range of technical solutions is identified which will meet those logical specifications. In other words in Stage 3 we have decided *what* we wish to do, whereas in Stage 4 we choose *how* it will be done. The users are normally presented with a number of options from which to make their choice. Because, at this stage, the details of where terminals will be sited, etc., are discussed, it is important to give a fairly wide group of users the opportunity to have a say in the final solution, since they may be directly affected by the new system.

In selecting the technical option the user is asked to consider aspects such as hardware (e.g. mainframe, mini, micros) and software environment. Some preliminary decisions may already have been made either during the feasibility study or while considering the Business Options. Frequently, existing equipment and/or software will restrict the number of options available. When producing the technical options it may prove necessary to diverge in some respects from the Business Option chosen earlier due to practical limitations. Indeed, as at this stage the cost/benefit analysis is produced in much greater depth, it may be desirable to review the selected Business System Option at the same time.

8.2 Define Technical Systems Options (Step 410)

As mentioned in the introduction to this chapter a lot of the information needed to complete this stage is outside the scope of SSADM and will require the analyst to interact with specialists in other areas to collate the necessary information to shape the TSO.

The aim is to produce three technical options for final consideration by the users. If no feasibility study has been carried out, however, it may be advisable to widen the scope of this stage by defining about six outline technical options initially and then, after discussions with the users, reduce these options to three.

The options are normally produced in outline from a 'brainstorming' session and should consider the following aspects:

- Are we going to need batch or on-line processing, or a mixture of the two?
- Will we need processing to be available at more than one point, in which case what levels of processing are needed and where are the processor(s) and terminals going to be located?
- Does data need to be passed between sites and, if so, what do we need?
- What software will need to be bought and/or developed?
- What staffing levels are required?
- What are the user interfaces?
- How will the system be developed and implemented?
- How will it actually meet the requirements in terms of functionality? For example, how will the reservations procedure actually be carried out?

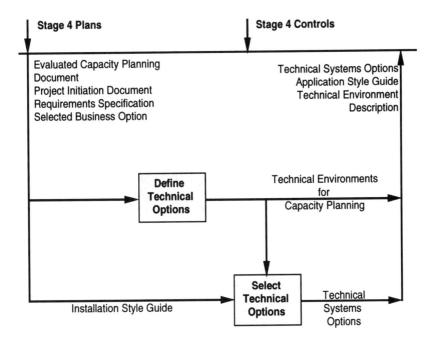

Figure 8.1 Steps and Tasks of Stage 4

8. 3 The Report

After the options have been identified in outline, a detailed report on each should be produced. These reports should look at the possible solutions under the following headings.

8.3.1 Technical Environment

The description given here should state the type, quantity and distribution of the hardware and software. Distribution of equipment needs careful consideration and although it should not be necessary to repeat the analysis already carried out, it is important to consider how the distribution will effect the running of the system. For example, if the system under consideration were an invoicing/stock control system, it would be very important to ensure that

1) there were sufficient terminals for all the staff involved in the area to have reasonable access to the data;
2) the software was able to support adequate response times at peak loading;
3) the production of invoices was not held up due to insufficient printers (or to the lack of a sufficiently large buffer in the printer or printers).

The way in which (large volumes of) data will be entered into the system should also be considered. Are there details from invoices/forms which have to be entered manually? How long is this likely to take? Does it tie up one terminal all the time? Should we consider an optical reader?

8.3.2 Functional Description

This should be provided in sufficient detail to show how the system will meet the requirements. The new system DFDs can be used here and any deviation from the requirements should be highlighted. For example, we may wish to indicate to the user that, in one of the options, reservations are entered at a terminal in each hotel and the details are held centrally, thus enabling the system to offer alternative accommodation if the particular hotel in question is fully booked.

8.3.3 Impact Analysis

Here we should detail how the new system will affect existing staff during and after implementation. If staff who are going to use the system are not consulted at this stage, there could be repercussions later when implementation is a reality. This section should also assess the advantages and disadvantages of the new system.

8.3.4 Outline Development Plan

This should show how the project will proceed in terms of timing and phasing, and should also include an estimate of the implementation date.

8.3.5 Cost/Benefit Analysis

The cost/benefit analysis may not be fully detailed as, at this stage, a particular supplier may not have been identified. In this case, an approximate figure should be used to give an idea of financial costs, as the purpose of this CBA is to provide a means of assessing each of the options.

8.4 Selection of Option (Step 420)

The report should now be presented formally to the users. This is an important step in SSADM in that the subsequent design process is based on the choice made at this point, and in order to ensure that the users have a full understanding of the implications of each system, a full presentation is required. It is also important to ensure that the users are given advice and support in making their decisions.

If the system is very complicated, it may be necessary to present each option separately. As with any presentation the users should be given the reports and possibly extracts from DFDs, etc., in time for them to digest the material properly. The presentation should follow the format of the report and plenty of time should be allowed for questions afterwards. Each presentation should be scheduled to last no longer than one hour.

8.5 Review Required System Specification

After the selection of an option by the user the solutions are added to the PRL and the DFDs, LDS, etc., because the new system produced in Stage 3 will have to be updated to reflect the chosen option.

Changes to the DFDs could include alteration of the system boundary, resulting in the inclusion/exclusion of a number of functions or changes to the processing within the functions.

The LDS could need amending to reflect the option, e.g. additional operational masters to meet access requirements and there may also be additions to the Entity Descriptions.

Changes to ELHs, Event Catalogue and Function Catalogues should be limited to the deletion of events not relevant to the chosen option or to changes in the type of processing, e.g. from batch to on-line.

The specification for the required system can now be consolidated and the revised outputs from Stage 2 should be included, together with a more detailed version of the report accompanying the option chosen by the user.

The final phase of this step is to produce a development plan for the remainder of the project. It is only the logical design phase (Stage 5) that can be planned in detail but outline plans for Stage 6 should be drawn up.

The plan should consider the following aspects:

- Detailed plan for next phase

- Detailed task list

- Estimates of time required to complete each task in terms of actual man days and elapsed time

- Detailed costing for the development of the next phase

- Procurement plan (if relevant)

- Programming plan containing:

    Resources required
    Timescales
    Workload

- System testing plan containing:

    Resources required
    Timescales

- Implementation plan containing:

    Description of conversion methods
    Description of change-over methods
    Estimates of resources and timescales

8.6 Define Design Objectives

The performance criteria for the system should be specified in this step. (Note that it is not essential to complete this step before embarking on Stage 5 as the performance objectives are not actually required until Stage 6.)

The areas which need to be addressed are:

- Information, i.e. what data is required?

- File space/utilisation

- Recovery

- Timing

The criteria are examined at this stage, primarily from the user's viewpoint: for example, acceptable user response time for each type of critical transaction. At the same time, the performance criteria also need to be discussed with personnel who are responsible for the hardware operation. The technical implications of these objectives will be examined in detail in Stage 6.

8.7 Conclusion

After the technical option has been selected, we are in a position to proceed with the detailed design of the new system. The logical design of the data and processing is addressed in Stage 5 respectively, and the physical design is then carried out in Stage 6.

9 Stage 5 : Logical Design

9.1 Introduction

This stage adds the specific detail of processing structures that were initially defined in the Requirements Specification and to specify the Human Computer Interface (HCI) in the form of dialogues. This detailed specification should

- be non-procedural

- be implementable on a range of technical environments

- maximise the opportunity for re-use

The three parts of this stage can be carried out in sequence or in parallel, this will depend on the skills and size of the project team.

9.2 Dialogue Design (Step 510)

This area of design is important to users as often they see their interaction with the system as synonymous with the functionality of the system. It is therefore imperative that they have a major role in this area of specification.

The design of the dialogues uses the structure notation broken down into dialogue elements. Each element represents a package of data items that are either inputs or outputs on the screen, forming the basis for screen design and physical dialogue design in Stage 6.

The information required for user dialogues is found in the function information associated with user interaction. The information is used to produce a structure for each dialogue and to define the menus and command structures.

Dialogue identification started with the User Catalogue in Stage 1 and developed into the User Roles in Stage 3. The identification is carried out by cross-reference of User Roles to functions in the User Role/Function Matrix (see Appendix 4); each match becomes a dialogue. For example, in the case study example, for security purposes only local or regional management can initiate the maintenance function, therefore the dialogue with that function is limited to the management role.

The User Role/Function Matrix should be discussed with the relevant users to ensure that the correct identification has been made.

9.2.1 Dialogue Element Description

Having completed the dialogue identification, the first activity is to produce a Dialogue Element Description for each dialogue. This lists the data items associated with the dialogue and is obtained from the Input/Output Structure associated with the Function Definition. Each dialogue element and the associated data items are listed on the Dialogue Element Description as shown in figure 9.2 in the two columns on the left hand side.

89

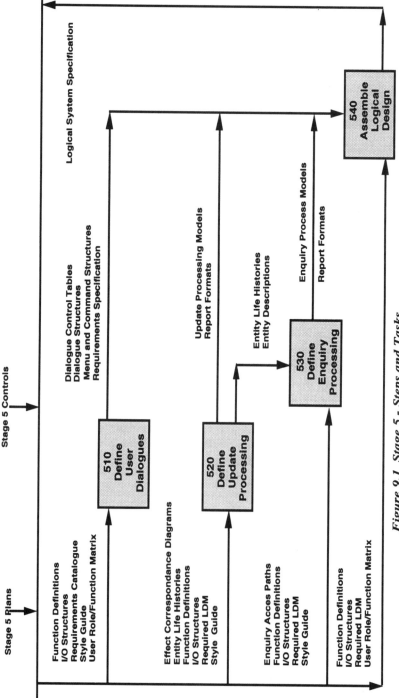

Figure 9.1 Stage 5 - Steps and Tasks

Dialogue Element Description : Receptionist/Accounts			
Dialogue Element	**Data Item**	**LGDE**	**M/O**
Departures Due	Date Guest_Surname Guest_Forenames Room_No	DEP_1	M/O
Accommodation Details	Guest_Surname Guest_Forenames Guest_Address Room_No Room_Type Tariff No_nights Accomm_Charge	BILL_1	M
Occupancy Details	Room_No Bar_Charges Rest_Charges	BILL_2	M
Special Rate Details	Special_Rate	BILL_3	O
Total Bill Details	Date Guest_Surname Guest_Forenames Guest_Address Room_No Room_Type No_nights Accomm_Charge Bar_Charge_Total Rest_Charge_Total Discount Total_Charge	BILL_4	M

Figure 9.2 Dialogue Element Description - Guest Departs

9.2.2 Logical Grouping of Dialogue Elements

Logical grouping of Dialogue elements (LGDE) is carried out to show navigation within the dialogue. This is done by examination of the Dialogue Structure, which is a copy of the I/O Structure fron the Function Definition.

This examination would normally be carried out with the users, as they would be most familiar with how the elements fit together in their work.

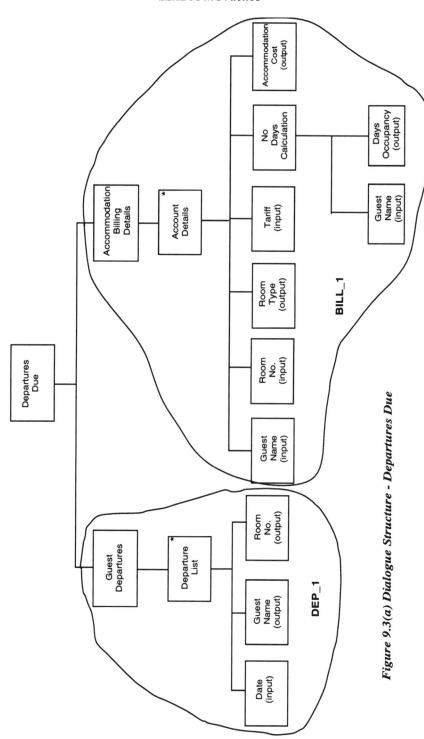

Figure 9.3(a) Dialogue Structure - Departures Due

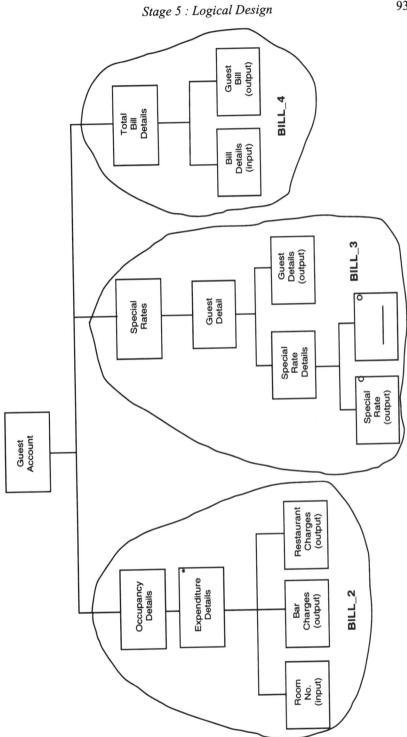

Figure 9.3(b) Dialogue Structure - Guest Accounts

The following are a guide to defining LDGEs.

- dialogue elements may be in sequence
- dialogue elements may be close together
- dialogue elements may not be separated from one another on the Dialogue Structure if the elements between are not part of the same grouping
- an element cannot be part of two groupings

The dialogue structure is then annotated (Figure 9.3(a and b)) to show the LGDE boundaries.

The next step is to add these LDGEs to the Dialogue Element Description, as shown in the third column of figure 9.2.

N.B. There are two Dialogue Structures for the example Function Definition in figures 9.3a and 9.3b. This is done to keep the diagrams concise and clear, there is a simple division in the function description where the elements shown in figure 9.3a are part of a function triggered automatically by the system date and the dialogue is between the system and the function. In figure 9.3b the elements are a dialogue between the user and the function.

9.2.3 Navigation between the Logical Groupings of Dialogue Elements

A Dialogue Control Table can now be constructed to identify the paths through the dialogue; an example can be found in Appendix 5. This table details the paths that can be taken through the dialogue in relation to each LDGE, listing the default path and all possible alternative routes. For example, it would show if an LDGE can be bypassed because the dialogue is optional.

The Dialogue Element Description can now have the Mandatory/Optional indicators added in column four. If the LGDE is a sequence, it will be mandatory. If it is a selection that contains a 'null' box it will be optional, otherwise mandatory, as the structure is indicating that one of the selections must be chosen. An LGDE that contains an iterative box can be mandatory or optional (M/O). Figure 9.2 illustrates a completed Dialogue Element Description.

9.2.4 Menu and Command Structures

Menu structures are a hierarchical structure that gives access to dialogues and off-line functions, and command structures show the control direction on completion of a dialogue. Thus the two structures provide a full design of all possible paths through the system as a whole.

9.2.5 Menu Structures

Menu construction is driven by referencing the User Role/Function Matrix. At the top level the functions that can be initiated by a user role are grouped together. In the case study this is a very small grouping, generally only one per role; however, in some systems this could range from one to all the dialogues in the system.

A hierarchical structure for the function groupings is now built, using a tree type structure, upwards from the initial grouping. The number of levels will depend on the number of dialogues to be organised. These groupings should be made with reference to the relevant users using the following guidelines and should incorporate any results from previous prototyping activities.

- groupings should reflect the way the user carries out the task (only the user can supply this information)
- groupings should consist of dialogues that belong together logically
- groupings at each level can consist of paths to lower level menus and direct routes to dialogues
- groupings do not have to have the same number of items

Examples of menu structures can be found in Appendix 5.

9.2.6 Command Structures

It is necessary to show the control path that can be taken on completion of a dialogue. This could be returning to a menu or moving directly to another dialogue, etc. The information required is once again most usefully obtained by discussions with the relevant user, but some assistance can be found on examination of the Function Definition. The type of option open to the user is

- return to the beginning of the dialogue
- return to the main menu
- to move to another dialogue

Figure 9.4 shows a Command Structure for the Receptionist/Accounts dialogue.

Command Control Structure : Receptionist/Accounts		
Option	**Dialogue or Menu**	**Dialogue/Menu Name**
Daily Departures	Menu	Accounts
Departure List	Menu	Daily Departures
Departures Due	Dialogue	DEP-1
Quit to Menu	Menu	Daily Departures
Charge Accommodation	Menu	Daily Departures
Accommodation Details	Dialogue	BILL_1
Quit to Menu	Menu	Accounts
Expenditure Charges	Menu	Accounts
Occupancy Details	Dialogue	BILL_2
Special Rate Details	Dialogue	BILL_3
Quit to Menu	Menu	Accounts
Finalise Account	Menu	Accounts
Final Bill Details	Dialogue	BILL_4
Quit to Menu	Menu	Accounts

Figure 9.4 : Command Structure - Receptionist/Accounts Dialogue

9.2.7 The Dialogue Design Products

The completed design for each dialogue will consist of a Dialogue Element Description, the Dialogue Structure, and a set of Command Structures (one for each dialogue). In addition there will be a Menu Structure for each User Role.

The dialogue design is carried out in close co-operation and consultation with the relevant users. As mentioned at the start of this section the user often perceives this element as the whole system, being unaware of the intricacies of the underlying functions; therefore, this is their view of the system's usability and it is of prime importance to the success of design that the users accept ownership in this area.

9.3 Define Update Processing (Step 520)

This step completes the specification of the update processing and the associated error handling. The information to make this development step is found in the Effect Correspondence Diagrams, ELHs, Function Descriptions and the Required LDM. During this stage the ELHs are enhanced with the addition of state indicators.

9.3.1 Modelling an Update Process

The procedure to specify an update process is carried out for every event that is identified during the Entity Life/Event Modelling.

A Jackson-like structure is built to model the process from the information gathered in the modelling steps. The example used in the following text is the 'Guest departs' event from the Case Study.

9.3.2 The Event

An event name should be unique, referring to the same event in the Function Definitions, ELH, ECD and Physical Process Specifications.

The event data is made up of the attributes input to the event; this would normally be the key of the entity that is the entry point to the LDM which has already been identified on the ECD, in addition to some of the updating information. This should be documented as a list showing any repeating groups in some sensible format, for example, by indenting in the list or the use of parenthesis, as with the previous examples in Chapter 6 for Relational Data Analysis.

At this point, each function including the event must be checked to ensure that the event data items are all included in the I/O Structure Diagrams or that they can be generated by the functions.

The output from the event, excluding error reports, must be listed even if it is a simple confirmation, i.e. 'Done'. If the output is less trivial it should be defined in the same way as an enquiry output (see section 9.4.4).

9.3.3 Enhancement of the Effect Correspondence Diagram

The ECD will have been completed in Stage 3 (see Chapter 7 Entity/Event modelling). This will now be utilised and enhanced in Stage 5.

The ECD may need to be extended to include 'enquiry only' entities where significant output from an event requires access to such entities. In those cases the ECD enhancement should follow procedures for Enquiry Process Modelling in section 9.4.

The effects on the ECD should now be grouped in a one-to-one correspondence by enclosing the groups in boxes; each box should then be named to reflect the process carried out.

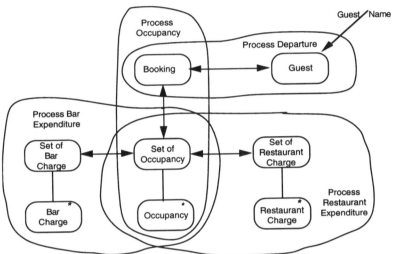

Figure 9.5 Enhanced Effect Correspondence Diagram - Guest Departs

9.3.4 Listing Operations

From each grouping the operations resulting from the event should now be listed, for each entity, in the following order (see Appendix 5 for 'Guest Departs' operations):

1. Read entity

2. Raise error on invalid state indicator

3. Create the entity

4. Operations from the effect on ELH need to be enhanced to provide more precise details. These enhancements will take the form of replacing the word 'entity' with the entity name and naming the attributes specifically. For example 'Store Keys of entity' will become 'Store Keys of Guest'.

5. Operation to set State Indicator, e.g. Set to <state indicator value>

6. Operation to write entity

Once the operations have been listed, the following validation checks can be carried out:

- For every Read there should be an error raising operation on every invalid state indicator.
- Every Store Key should be preceded by a Create operation.
- If a State Indicator or attribute is changed by an operation there should be an equivalent Write operation for that entity.

9.3.5 Conversion to a Jackson-like Structure

The ECD with the grouped effects can now be converted to a Jackson-like structure diagram; the Figure 9.6 shows the converted ECD from Figure 9.5.

Having converted the ECD the operations from the Operations List can now be added to the structure diagram. The operations are allocated to the appropriate process node, i.e. the process nodes that represent the effect to which the operation applies, as illustrated in Figure 9.6. To maintain a logical order the operations should be allocated a number in the same sequence as the operations list was constructed for the ELH.

9.3.6 Allocation of Conditions to Structure

Conditions are allocated above each option within a selection and each iterated node. These conditions often test the State Indicator value of the entity and in the iteration case 'end_of_data_set'.

9.3.7 Specify Error Outputs

For every error detected, a suitable error message should be generated; such messages should be designed in such a way that the user receiving the message will know what is wrong and how to correct it. For this reason the user should be involved in this area of development.

9.3.8 Checking the Process

Now that the structure is complete, the resulting process should be checked to ensure that the sequencing is correct. One of the most effective quality methods is a 'structured walk-through', i.e. with relevant users and the diagram, go through the process step by step carefully using example data.

9.3.9 Integrity Errors

Any system must maintain the integrity of the database, i.e. the data must be consistent; also included in that integrity will be the rules of the Organisation. For example in the Case Study, an entity should not exist that has not been updated for two years.

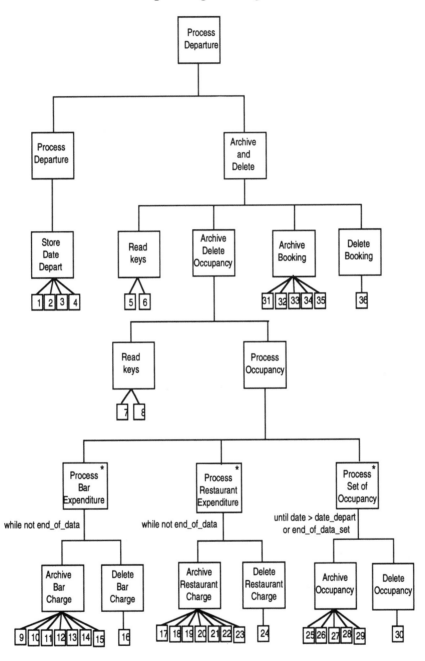

Figure 9.6 Update Process Structure - Guest Departs

N.B. The Operations for this Updates Process Structure are shown in Appendix 5.

In order to maintain this integrity the analyst should include, as part of the specification of integrity errors, statements that cause process failure if an entity is not in a valid state. This applies to both update and enquiry processes.

9.4 Define Enquiry Process (Step 530)

This step completes the database Enquiry Process specification and associated error handling. The enquiries are found in the I/O Structures and the Enquiry Access Paths documented in Stage 3 during Logical Data Modelling and Dialogue Design.

9.4.1 Modelling an Enquiry Process

As with the Update Process the Enquiry name must be unique. Other areas of the modelling differ substantially from that of the Update process, although in some circumstances the Update Process modelling needs to incorporate some of these techniques (see 9.3.3). Essentially, the output part of the I/O Structure is merged with the EAP to produce a Jackson-like structure for each enquiry.

9.4.2 Enquiry Triggers

An enquiry trigger consists of the data items input to the enquiry; this would normally be the key of the entity that is the point of entry to the LDM and which has already been identified on the EAP. In addition, there may be selection criteria that determine the details retrieved. This trigger should be documented as a list of data items on the Enquiry Access Path; in the case of repeating groups as a separate Jackson-like structure. The same check must be carried out as with the Update Function to ensure that every data item is contained in, or can be derived by, the functions containing the enquiry.

9.4.3 Enquiry Output

The output for an enquiry is extracted from the I/O Structures of any function that contains that enquiry, simply by removing those parts of the structure which concern input from the user. If the data comprising output, excluding error messages, contains a repeating group it will be documented as a Jackson-like structure. If there is no repeating group it is sufficient to document as a simple list of data items.

It should be noted that if the I/O Structure diagram has mainly 'output' boxes, then very few, if any, changes are required. It is convention that an output structure is constructed; however, in some cases this would be a duplication of the I/O structure, as in the case of 'Guest Accounts' in the Case Study.

9.4.4 Group Access on Enquiry Path

The accesses on the EPD diagram are grouped in a similar way to the ECD in Update Process Definition on a one-to-one correspondence (section 9.3.2).

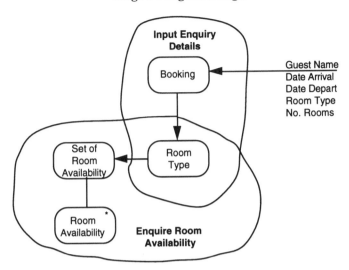

Figure 9.7 Enhanced Enquiry Access Path - Booking Enquiry

9.4.5 Conversion to a Jackson-like Structure

Each elementary and grouped access on the enhanced EPD are represented by a node. Extra nodes may have to be inserted to conform to the Structuring Rules (see Chapter 6).

9.4.6 Input and Output Data Structure Correspondence

At this point in the procedure we have one diagram that represents the inputs and one that represents the outputs. The correspondence between nodes on these two structures must now be examined. Differences in structure may occur and it is at this point of development that they will be revealed. If there is a difference between the I/O Structure view of the output and the database view, it will usually be resolved at this stage by defining additional processes to sort and format the data appropriately.

To examine the correspondences, put both structures side by side, and look for corresponding nodes.

Where a correspondence has been shown merge the two nodes as a single process, then redraw the diagram to form a Process Structure as shown in Figure 9.8.

9.4.7 List and Allocate Operations

With an Enquiry Process only read operations are allocated in Stage 5; any other operations will be dealt with in Stage 6.

List the operations and allocate them to the appropriate node on the structure.

9.4.8 Allocate Conditions

Conditions are added above selection options; these often test State Indicator values, and iterated components where the test is often 'end_of_data_set'.

9.4.9 Specification of Errors

See section 9.3.8 for details of integrity Errors. Fail conditions are included in the list of operations after the read operation on an entity.

Error outputs should follow the same pattern as for Update Processes.

9.4.10 Checking Enquiry Process

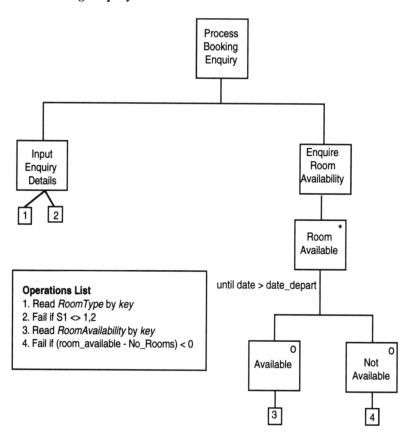

Operations List
1. Read *RoomType* by *key*
2. Fail if S1 <> 1,2
3. Read *RoomAvailability* by *key*
4. Fail if (room_available - No_Rooms) < 0

Figure 9.8 Enquiry Process Structure - Booking Enquiry

The procedure of structured walk-through with the user is suggested as the best method of checking correctness of sequencing.

9.5 Conclusion

If all the necessary products have been passed accurately from Stage 3 (Requirements Specification), the Logical Design Stage is very much a question of following procedures. There are of course many pitfalls for the inexperienced analyst, and therefore more in-depth reading in the area of Database Design and Interface is recommended.

This stage is completed by assembling all the relevant products, Dialogue Designs, Update Process Specifications and Enquiry Process Specification and passing them through to the final SSADM stage of the project.

10 Stage 6: Design of the Physical System

10.1 Introduction

Stage 6 of SSADM is concerned with converting the logical design of the new system into a physical design specification. The logical design of the system, as we have seen, is a product of Stage 5 where we produce the logical Update and Enquiry Process Structures and the Dialogue Design.

In the SSADM Manual there is recognition that the Physical Design stage can become so product specific that it would be outside of the realms of SSADM. What Stage 6 does is present a generic set of design aspects that can be used as a guide to the Physical Design Process.

The stage requires expertise in the form of designers, programmers and other specialists in the area of Physical Design Strategy and Processing System Specification. Analysts can specify function components, but experienced designers are required to decide how those components can be implemented.

In this stage, as with all others, user representatives must be involved to confirm acceptance (that the users accept ownership of the system) of the design and implementation; this is for validation, but is also important to ease the eventual acceptance of the implemented system.

This chapter will outline the Physical Process Specification as an overview of the generic aspects. This stays within the book's philosophy of being written as a guide for people new to analysis and SSADM, since detailed design would be outside the scope of the book as well as the experience of the expected readership. Readers are encouraged to supplement their reading of this chapter with study of the SSADM Physical Design sections of the Manual.

It is worth bearing in mind that although we selected the hardware and software configuration that we intended to use in Stage 4, it is not until now that the final decisions have to be made. It may be that between Stages 4 and 5 and reaching Stage 6 external constraints have changed, so we may need to review the choice at this point.

In SSADM version 4 it has been recognised that the physical design approach needs to be tailored to the specific environment of the project, but that the activities in this stage will take place in some way whatever the environment. The steps within the stage should therefore be regarded as guidelines which are then tailored to the specific environment.

The steps are illustrated in Figure 10.1. Which steps are taken will very much depend on the environment for development, for example if no procedural code is required then Step 650 (Complete Function Specification) becomes optional. Using a 4GL will allow the system to be generated after Step 630, while using a 3GL, coding will wait until after Step 670.

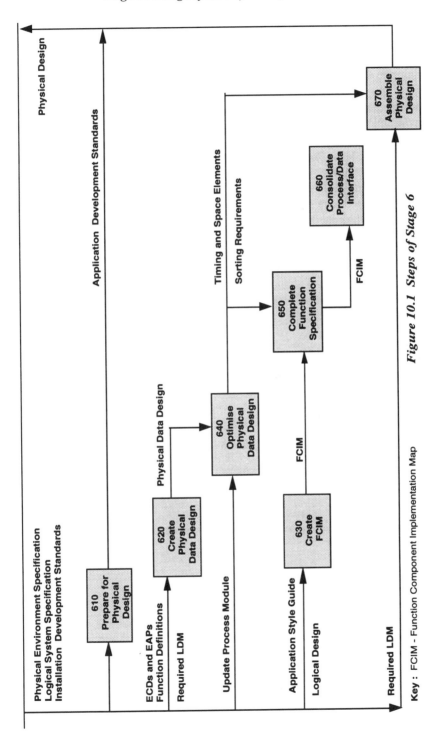

Figure 10.1 Steps of Stage 6

Key : FCIM - Function Component Implementation Map

10.2 Preparing for Physical Design (Step 610)

Step 610 can start as soon as the implementation environment is known. The physical environment must be examined and the important characteristics pertaining to data storage, performance and the processing system are defined. The definitions of these elements are carried out using the physical environment specification (documentation passed into the stage from the project management environment), and usually with the assistance of a designer well versed in the specific physical environment. The information from this study is collated onto a form that classifies the processing system facilities (Physical Environment Classification) including: tools available; type of language(s); type of process handling; dialogue processing and navigation; error handling facilities.

Initially, the design team studies documentation related to the selected DBMS to complete the data design element of the Physical Environment Classification. SSADM has two forms on which this information can be noted, the DBMS Data Classification form, how data is stored and retrieved, and the DBMS Performance Classification form, how data can be accessed and the updating properties. (Examples of these can be found in the SSADM Manual.)

Once these forms have been completed the designer can document space and timing estimations that reflect the facilities available in the DBMS.

10.3 Create Physical Design Strategy (Step 620)

Step 620 defines how the Logical Specification can be mapped onto the implementation environment and will include

- Processing System Classification

- DBMS Data Storage Classification

- DBMS Performance Classification

Once the strategy has been outlined the Physical Design of Data and Processing can begin. These two tasks, although identified separately, are interdependent and information needs to be freely passed from one to the other throughout the development period.

10.4 Overview of Physical Data and Process Design

The design process tends to take place in the following way:
1) The Required System LDM is converted to an 'unoptimised universal' data model; this then has product specific rules applied to it and is modified, as appropriate.

2) The Function Component Implementation Maps (FCIM) are now constructed.

3) The data design is optimised by referring to the FCIM and data and performance objectives in the Required System Model.

4) If a procedural language is being used the Function Definitions must be completed.

5) Finally the interface between processing and the database is defined.

10.5 Physical Data Design

The first step in physical data design is to take the 'logical' data model and produce a 'first cut' physical data design. Reference will be made to the LDM, EAPs, ECDs, and Entity Descriptions from the Required System Specification.

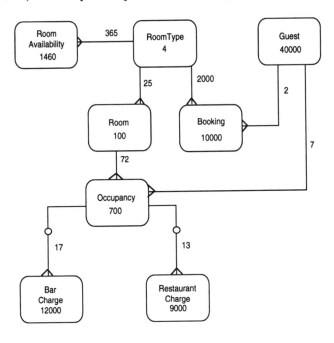

Figure 10.2 : Physical Data Structure - First Step

10.5.1 Identify Relevant Features of Required LDM

The Physical Data Model does not replace the required LDS and not all the information on the required LDS is needed to construct the physical data model. The difference between the information on the Required LDS and the physical data design can be summarised as

• Relationship Optionality is only required where a master must exist for a detail entity; this is to determine where to place non-root entities when deciding physical groups, i.e. Mandatory detail to Master relationships.

• Design Volumes - the number of occurrences of each entity (number in box) and the dependent occurrences (numbers at crow's feet); how many detail entities per master entity.

• Relationship names are not used

• An exclusion arc on a relationship is not used in this context.

By following this set of criteria and applying them to the Case Study Required LDS the diagram shown in figure 10.2 can be produced as a first version of the physical data design.

10.5.2 Identify Entry Points

Entry points should be allocated for any entity that is accessed directly during an update or enquiry process. These points will be found by examination of the ECDs and EAPs produced in Stage 3.

Entry point attributes should be annotated on the Physical Data Structure; if an access is not via a primary key, the item should be enclosed in a circle.

10.5.3 Roots of Physical Groups

The annotation for a root entity is a bar across the top of the box, as shown in Figure 10.3.

A root is identified by applying one of the following criteria
  a) Is the entity without a master?
  b) Is the entity an entry point?

The exception to b) is an entity that has a composite or compound key, one part of which is the primary key to an entity already defined as a root. In this case the entity with the compound or composite key is not marked as a root.

Figure 10.3 shows the Case Study physical data design after the addition of entry points and roots.

10.5.4 Identify Allowable Physical Groups

Entities that are not roots now have to be allocated to a root entity; this is in order to form the physical groupings of data. The allocation to a group is based on the following

a) An entity is placed in same group as its mandatory master.

b) Where more than one master exists, place with the master whose key is part of the entity's own key.

Where an entity still has an unresolved grouping the next activity will provide the solution.

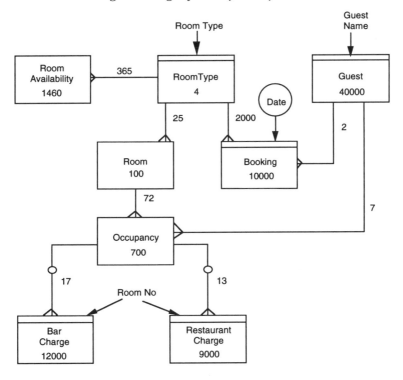

Figure 10.3 : Physical Data Design - Second Step

10.5.5 Least Dependent Occurrence

If in the previous activity an entity could be allocated to more than one group, the entity is placed in the root group in which it occurs least. The Physical Data Structure with the groups is shown in Figure 10.4.

10.5.6 Block and Group Size

Firstly, the block size which is used by the system software should be determined. This would normally be set by the selected DBMS; if not, the designer must choose the most efficient size. This should be a balance between maximising the volume of data handled and minimising the buffer sizes for block transfer. The second task is to measure the group size against the block size; this involves calculating the lengths of all the attrributes for the entities in the group, multiplying them by the approximate number of occurrences and adding an allowance for indexes, etc.

If a Physical Group does not fit the block size, the group must be split until the resulting groups are less than, or equal to, the block size.

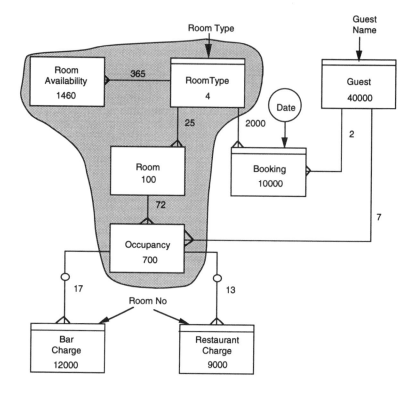

Figure 10.4 Physical Data Structure

10.5.7 Product Specific Rules

The Physical Data Design must now be mapped to the facilities provided by the DBMS; these facilities will be found in the DBMS Data Storage Classification Document. It should be mentioned at this point that many DBMS permit the direct implementation of an LDS; in this case only 10.4.1 needs be carried out by the analyst.

10.6 Space and Performance

If the previous activities have been completed, the design may need to be modified to meet the required storage and performance objectives within the RC and Function Definitions. The design must be tested using either paper-based calculations or tools supplied with the DBMS.

In optimising the design the space and performance efficiency issues are balanced against the need to keep the data structure as close as possible to the Required LDM, for reasons of maintenance, flexibility and understanding of the design. The tasks involved in optimisation require a thorough knowledge of the implementation environment; failing that, sophisticated tools are needed to carry out optimisation.

Some issues which can be considered in optimisation are:

• Restructuring the design to fit storage constraints. This can be done in a number of ways; for example use of codes instead of full names, redesign to remove redundancy, or reduced levels of historical data.

• Identify functions that will be critical to performance. These will normally be frequently used functions that work with high volumes of data or access large numbers of entity occurrence. Using the DBMS Data storage Classification Document the time taken by any critical function should be estimated and checked against the RC and Function Definitions. If there are differences, that means the objectives cannot be achieved, and decisions will need to be made as to how to improve performance on access time.

• Examining other alternatives, such as introducing controlled redundancy by adding a data item to an entity in order to save an access on another entity. Calculations could be stored instead of being carried out on every access. An alternative DBMS may improve performance, or the performance objectives could be altered if the discrepancy is small.

If changes are made, then the timing tests must be repeated until the performance objectives are satisfied. Once the data has been optimised the Physical Data Design needs only tidying up to be complete. This will involve

• validation of sequencing imposed by design

• documentation of any sorting requirements

• updating Function Definitions and RC to reflect any changes to requirements

• documenting optimisation

10.7 Physical Process Specification

When specifying the physical processes the logical design products are converted into programs, physical I/O formats and physical dialogue designs that will work in the selected physical environment. As with the physical data design, this involves mapping the logical products to the implementation environment. This is a more difficult task and SSADM offers guidelines to the designer that address the generic issues in making this conversion.

The processing environment has been defined at the start of Stage 6 and decisions about the process specification must take account of the constraints and strengths of this environment.

There are three steps involved in the physical process specification

Step 630 - Create Function Component Implementation Map (FCIM)

Step 650 - Complete Function Specification

Step 660 - Consolidate Process Data Interface

The following sections will outline the activities and their purpose without exploring the finer detail.

10.8 Function Component Implementation Map (FCIM)

Functions were initially defined during Stage 3, in Stage 6 these functions must be implemented. The function definitions are now mapped onto the specific implementation environment in terms of fragments. By fragmenting the functions, reusable elements can be recognised.

An FCIM is developed for each function. The form of an FCIM is not defined and will be decided for any project in the Physical Design Strategy. It could for example be a network diagram or simply a list of components. These components will include operations, events, enquiries, entity groups, dialogues, physical screens, error and control handling.

The activities we will consider are those that will be performed by a designer regardless of the specific physical implementation environment. Some of these activities are ongoing (removal of duplication and common processing) and some are applied to each function. These activities are outlined in the following sections.

10.8.1 Removal of Duplication

There are two areas that can be examined for duplication.

1. If an Enquiry Process Model is followed immediately by an Update Process Model that acts on the same data, check if

    • the trigger for the enquiry is a subset of the event data

    • the enquiry process is a sub-set of the update process

    If this is the case the the Enquiry Process Model should be discarded and the Update Process Model can be implemented to include the enquiry dialogue.

    For example in the Case Study, the Booking Enquiry Model could be designed in the first instance with a Booking Update Process Model following, carrying out the step above would mean that the two processes could be implemented by merging them into one.

2. Where an Enquiry Process preceding an Update Process is simply a duplication of part or all of the Update Process with the exclusion of update operations, the situation should come under closer examination. This may be a reasonable design decision; however, there are overheads that could make it a bad decision. For example, if the enquiry process does not have validation tests, then the user can become alienated from the system if work is rejected because of validation failure in the Update Process.

Returning to the Case Study Booking Enquiry Process, let us say that on interrogating the system for room availability on certain dates the resulting data is not validated and an offer based on that data is made to the potential guest. On acceptance by the potential guest the data is accessed again; however this time, being an update process the data integrity is checked and the update request fails. The result will be not only be an inconvenience to the user but also to the potential guest.

10.8.2 Identification of Common Processing

Some common processing will have already been identified at the event and enquiry level and noted on the Function Descriptions. Others may have been discovered from processes on the DFDs and documented on the EPDs. As development of the system continues identification of this type is annotated on the EPDs with the event, function or enquiry name that utilises the process.

Further areas of common processing can be identified at this stage and the areas to be scrutinised are

- events shared between functions

- operations that are the same across events

- the same calculations used by different events

- situations where similar sets of entities are accessed

There are many reasons why code should be developed in a modular way, encouraging the reuse of physical fragments. Great care must be exercised by the designer to ensure that what appears to be a common process also has identical requirements in all instances of use.

10.8.3 Define Success Units

The success unit is a set of processing that either succeeds or fails as a whole; in design terms it defines the way data will be presented to the function to complete all the changes of state for each affected entity, as illustrated by the state indicators on the ELH.

A function may have a number of success units and they generally only apply to update functions.

These success units are examined at this stage because the logical units may not be implementable in the physical environment for several reasons

- they lock the database for too long

- they impose performance constraints

- as a commit unit they are too large for the implementation DBMS

If we take the example of a central booking system for a large chain of hotels, the system needs to respond quickly to input and also maintain up-to-date room availability details. If the complete booking process has just one success unit, then the records affected by that booking will be locked and unavailable to other users for the entire booking process. Alternatively, if the room booking details are presented as one success unit, and then the other booking details as a separate success unit, room availability can be updated and the lock released for other users, thus allowing the further booking details to be completed as another success unit.

10.8.4 Syntax Error Handling

This is an error detected in the input data. Specification of these syntactic errors is left until Stage 6, firstly to avoid an unnecessary level of detail in logical data definition and secondly because they are more easily specified by using the method available in the physical environment.

In non-procedural language the syntactic errors can be specified by either storing with the data item in the physical database specification, or with the data item in the physical input data specification, for instance in the screen definition. If an error is specific to a particular function it must be specified using the second method.

Error messages should be stored in the database to ease maintenance and allow reuse of the message by multiple processes.

The following are examples of syntactic error specification contained in a physical database specification

data item : room_number
error condition : not in the range 1-376
error message : Invalid room_number

10.8.5 Controls and Control Error

The input and update controls should be documented in the RC; they fall into two categories, correct use of functions (navigation) and control of data errors.

Correct use of functions can be achieved by implementing limited access to the function.

Control in data errors can be applied by checking data with various algorithms, checksums, hashing and check digits for example. The error reporting can require re-input of data or the abortion of the function.

10.8.6 Physical Input/Output Formats

The physical I/O formats can be divided into two parts, those related to dialogues and those related to reports.

1. Dialogues

Dialogues have been designed during the logical system specification, these designs must now be mapped to the physical screens; physical data groups; the input view of physical data groups; extending dialogue components to include error handling; navigation paths through the dialogues.

The designer will be able to use the Application Development Standards to assist in this step, as this includes such information as standard menu layout, where errors should appear on a screen, standard navigation methods, etc.

Further reading of specific areas of design of physical dialogues is recommended; the SSADM Manual provides a more detailed study.

2. Reports, Input and Output Files

Physical design will add many constraints to these elements of I/O design. For example devices such as printers, screens, tapes and disc force limitations on the format of I/O that they can handle. Softer device issues addressing message handling or file transfer must also be examined.

This area is of prime importance to the user as the user interface design must conform to any required standards and user acceptance of the design is vital to the implemented system's success.

Care must also be taken to ensure that any I/O accessing external systems conform to the required standards for the external devices.

10.8.7 Complete the Function Specification (Procedural/Non-procedural)

The skill required in this step is that of an experienced designer. Even in a physical environment where specification has followed the non-procedural language path there are often instances where programs cannot match the processing standard templates and procedural code needs to be inserted to complete the process.

A physical database process that has been generated with non-procedural code can sometimes have an unacceptable performance level and this may be improved by writing the process in a procedural language.

When a function needs to be specified partly or wholly in a procedural way then the designer must further specify the process especially in relation to modularity, i.e. how the logical processes can be implemented as physical modules and combined together.

If the implementation can be achieved using only non-procedural language the broad outline achieved by taking the previous steps to produce an FCIM will be sufficient.

Again, the reader is referred to the SSADM Manuals for further information.

10.9 Conclusion

As mentioned at the start of the chapter, this stage is very dependent on the implementation environment. In some cases this stage will require experts in the environment to analyse the products and produce the Physical Design. As with Stage 4 (Technical Options) much of the material, the Project Standards and

Application Style Guide will have been created at a project management level, giving guidance to the analyst in completing the System.

What this chapter has tried to do is to show the activities involved in the stage and give the reader a feel for the tasks involved in Physical Process Design. The conclusion that may be drawn by the student new to Systems Analysis is that the skills involved are wide ranging, from the ability to communicate with all manner of people to highly developed technical knowledge. All the techniques can be learnt and assimilated but, for many of the skills required, only time and experience will develop and expand the areas of knowledge.

As stated in the introduction to this chapter the information required to carry out Stage 6 is specific to the physical implementation environment and therefore the explanations are restricted to the generic issues. It should also be pointed out that in many cases SSADM stops at Stage 5 (or sometimes even Stage 4) because the dictates of the physical implementation environment make other physical development options a better way to complete the development process.

11 SSADM - A Critique

SSADM has now been widely used for a number of years and some doubts have been expressed about its contribution to the successful development of information systems. In this chapter an attempt is made to review these criticisms and generally evaluate the method.

11.1 Scope

A number of aspects of the system development life cycle are considered as outside the scope of SSADM. Strategic planning of information systems, for example, which is an integral part of some other structured methods, most notably Information Engineering, is excluded from SSADM, although the method presumes that it is addressed by organisations using another (unspecified) approach. Similarly, some aspects of design such as the human computer interface are not discussed and again the presumption is that such matters will be covered elsewhere. Although this may not be an unreasonable assumption, it is perhaps surprising to realise that an analyst who was trained exclusively in SSADM would lack a number of fundamental skills.

It is also difficult to deny that SSADM still seems to be founded on the use of 3rd generation programming languages rather that 4GL environments. Despite the revisions to the latter stage and, in the authors' view, the transition from analysis to design is still both over-complex and imprecise.

11.2 Complexity

The all-encompassing nature of SSADM can be considered both its strength and weakness. By providing a very detailed step-by-step guide to systems analysis and design, the method aims to give a clear definition of the role of the analyst at each stage in the life cycle of the project. Additionally, a key point of the method is that the techniques and documentation should be used to cross check each other at various points in the analysis and design process.

One of the results of such a comprehensive approach is that, for the person newly exposed to SSADM, it can appear both over-complex and confusing. In particular, it can be difficult to gain an overall feel for the method, or to understand how the various stages and techniques fit together. The authors hope that this book will have allayed at least some of these misgivings, but nonetheless it may well be that the method could benefit from simplification in some directions.

In practice the method, like any other, should be applied with common sense and with due regard to the type and scale of the project involved. The authors suggest that any installation considering SSADM should firstly review its suitability as a method, bearing in mind that SSADM was designed with large-scale projects in mind and in particular to deal with the problems of continuity and control caused by such projects. Secondly, the stages and techniques should be examined as to their appropriateness for each project and brief guidelines issued at the commencement of each project.

11.3 Cost

The introduction of a new analysis and design approach inevitably has a number of 'hidden' costs; for example, training costs; the need to maintain traditionally designed systems and hence to maintain traditional skills; demotivation of staff employed on traditional projects, etc. Generally, structured methods also lengthen the analysis phase of a project and this can prove difficult to sell to the users.

The proponents of SSADM, like those of other structured methods, claim that the gains made in terms of accuracy, flexibility and robustness of design, more than offset these disadvantages. Furthermore, a compensating reduction in the time taken for the design phase of a project should usually be expected. However, these claims have yet to be proved and doubt has been expressed in many quarters regarding the cost effectiveness of SSADM.

11.4 Other Approaches to Analysis and Design

11.4.1 Prototyping

Version 4 of SSADM has attempted to incorporate prototyping (for specification purposes) into the method. However, in the authors' view the approach is far from satisfactory in that the steps are so prescriptive that they appear almost to contradict the principles behind prototyping. Although according to some critics, the two approaches are incompatible, it is our view that prototyping has much to offer SSADM (and vice versa) and it is hoped that the next release of the method will further address this issue.

11.4.2 Object Oriented Analysis and Design

Version 4 of SSADM was released when OOD was a relatively new approach and consequently SSADM does not reflect any of the object oriented developments. However, it is intended that the next release of SSADM will specifically incorporate object orientation.

11.4.3 Further Developments

It has to be recognised that one disadvantage of a relatively rigorous approach as represented by SSADM is that it is likely to adapt more slowly (and with more difficulty) to new developments. However, it is perhaps unfortunate that revisions of SSADM appear to be so infrequent. The result of such delays is that practitioners must inevitably develop their own solutions/approaches unless they are prepared to forgo any advantage offered by new replacements.

11.5 Quality Considerations

SSADM Version 4 claims to define quality criteria for its analysis and design products and also presumes that quality assurance reviews take place at the end of each stage. However, possibly like some other quality systems, despite its intentions it cannot offer any guarantee of quality. For example, users may sign off a stage without having understood the products and/or noticing all errors or omissions. It is therefore essential that analysts should not only use constant informal reviews with users but also continuously apply their own critical faculties to the work they produce. The authors would moreover like to see a post implementation review become a mandatory step in the method!

11.6 Conclusion

SSADM does have a number of critics who argue that it is both a costly and outdated approach to analysis and design. Such critics appear to have gained ground in that SSADM is no longer mandatory within government departments. Rather, such departments are now being encouraged to select the method they consider most appropriate to the project in question. It remains to be seen however whether the result is a return to anarchy and chaos or an improvement in quality and cost effectiveness.

Appendix 1 - The Case Study

Introduction

This case study has been used throughout the book to provide examples of the SSADM techniques. This set of appendices contains an example set of the SSADM documentation produced for the Hotel System concerned.

A Case Study cannot always, as in real life, supply examples of all products, but we have tried to choose a study that will allow students of SSADM to understand the basic techniques without overburdening them with complexities as they start out. There is no substitute for practice and experience in the world of system analysis; what we hope to provide is a basic reference set of documentation to start the reader on the right path.

The appendices present our view of the system as it goes through the various stages of development. We would take this opportunity to reiterate the point that in system development there is no absolutely right answer, although there can of course be wrong answers. When studying the products in the appendices students may differ in their view of the system. We would see any resulting discussion as a good learning experience and an ideal use of the Case Study material.

Case Study Background

The case study concerns a large hotel chain based in the UK, the Serve You Right Hotels Group.

The group consists of 28 hotels, organised on a regional basis as follows: 4 in Central London, 6 in the South East, 5 in the South West, 4 each in the Midlands and the North West, 3 in the North East and 2 in Scotland.

Each hotel has between 40 and 100 bedrooms, which are categorised as double (D), twin(T), single(S), or luxury(L). Double and twin rooms may be let as singles. All bedrooms have private bathrooms, colour television, hairdryers, etc. There are no central systems, so each hotel has its own reservation and billing systems and forwards occupancy statistics to regional headquarters on a monthly basis. A new group managing director has recently been appointed. One of the director's major objectives is to increase the level of central control by standardising as many of the hotel procedures as possible and by automating the reporting procedures from hotels to regional and group/central headquarters. The director has therefore appointed a firm of consultants to investigate and define the IT requirements of the company.

Project Initiation Document

In this example a complete template for a P.I.D. used by a respected consultancy group is employed. For the purposes of the case study not all the information has been completed, as much of it is not SSADM but a surrounding Project Management System which falls outside the remit of this book. However, it is important to recognise that these areas of information are required and that SSADM cannot stand by itself without a project management framework to surround the analysis work.

Project Initiation Document

Name of project :   Reservations and Billing
                            Phase One
Initiator :   Ms. I. Startit
                            Group Managing Director
                            Serve-You-Right Hotels

1: Business Case

1.1 Justification

An initial examination of the existing systems of reservations, billing and communication of management information suggests that a number of changes including a relatively simple implementation of information technology could achieve the following.

1.1.1 Benefits

   a) Improve the accuracy of reservations and billing

   b) Increase the level of customer service

   c) Improve the level of management information at group and regional level.

These three benefits would combine to improve individual hotel and group efficiency. The increased level of customer service is essential to survive in an increasingly competitive industry and better and more accurate levels of management information will enable better informed and faster decision taking; this should have an efficiency and productivity feed-back, which in the long term should provide greater profit margins.

1.1.2 Anticipated Costs, Timescales and Constraints

   Anticipated Costs -

   Timescales - pilot running in six months

   Constraints -

2: Project Brief

2.1 Project Objectives

The project is concerned with the reservations and billing procedures of the Serve-You-Right chain of hotels. The investigation is to include existing procedures within the hotels, using the Blacksands venue as the model, the operating needs of these individual hotels and the requirements of the regional and central headquarters.

   The objective of the study is to recommend improvements to the reservations and billing procedures so that :

Accurate management information is available more quickly and more cheaply by reducing clerical effort. Customer service is improved by faster production of bills. Revenue loss is reduced by improving the accuracy of customer bills.

2.2 Project End Products

The project documentation will conform to the SSADM Version 4 Standards.

2.2.1 End Product Checklist

Stage 1	Project Management Documentation
	Current Services Description
	Requirements Catalogue
	User Catalogue
Stage 2	Business System Options
	Selected Business System Option
Stage 3	Requirements Specification
Stage 4	Project Management Documentation
	Technical System Option
Stage 5	Logical Design
Stage 6	Project Management Documentation
	Physical Design

2.2.2 Product Descriptions

For the case study this is not included, as examples of all SSADM products, except RDA, are included. In a real system development the developers may have elected to omit some elements from a specified product as unecessary or unsuitable for the project. The product descriptions will include any element that is included in the resultant product from a stage of development.

2.3 Project Constraints

Billing procedures are only to be included in so far as they affect the reception's activities. Subsequent accounting activities are excluded.

   Any recommendations should allow for a 10% annual increase in bookings over the next five years and for an additional ten hotels to be added to the group.

3: Project Boundary

3.1 Functional Boundary

The individual hotels' reception activities and the collation of management information.

3.2 Interproject Relationships

There is no other project at this time; however, the possibility of communications links between hotels, regional and group offices at a later date should influence the resulting design.

3.3 IT Security Risk Boundary

Responsibility for the information will in the first instance stay within the individual hotel; however, in relation to the above requirement that inter hotel-region-group communications may be installed at some later date, consideration to the increased risk should be given at this time.

4: Project Management

4.1 Key Staff and Responsibilities

    4.1.1 Project Board
    4.1.2 Project Management
    4.1.3 Project Assurance
    4.1.4 Project Team

4.2 Project Plans

4.3 Quality Policy

    4.3.1 Quality Control
    4.3.2 Quality Review Attendees
    4.3.3 Quality Review Schedule

4.4 Controls

    4.4.1 Project Board Meeting
    4.4.2 Highlight Reports
    4.4.3 Checkpoint Meetings

5: Financial Control

    5.1 Project Costs
    5.2 Source of Funds
    5.3 Authorisation

6: Additional Information

An outline of the current reservations and billing procedures for the Serve You Right hotel at Blacksands follows.

Reservations and Billing System in the Serve-You-Right Hotel, Blacksands

When a guest make an enquiry about booking a room or rooms, the reservations clerk checks the reservations diary to see whether a room of the right type is available on the date(s) required. If not, alternative date(s)/room types are offered to the guest. If a booking is made, the reservations clerk records in pencil in the diary the customer's name, address and telephone number, name of the company if appropriate, and the room type required against the first day of the booking. The figure in the diary for the number of rooms available for that room type for that day is decreased. If the booking is for more than one day, the guest's surname is recorded against the subsequent days and the room total adjusted. In a few cases a guest requests a particular room or particular requirements. Such requests are noted in the diary. Once a letter of confirmation is received from the guest the pencilled entry ishas inked in and the letter placed in the customer file (by the reservations clerk) customer files are stored alphabetically in the filing cabinet. If the visit is the first by this customer, a customer record is then also completed. Reservations may be made by a company rather than an individual, in which case the same procedures are followed, except that all the customer information is referenced and filed by the company name. Bookings which are unconfirmed after three days are disregarded if the room is required by another guest.

Every morning the reservations clerk checks the diary and forwards an arrivals list to reception. Reception checks the customer file for any special requirements, and allocates a room number using the room chart which shows the type, location and availability of each room in the hotel. This room number is and added to the arrivals list and a daily rooms list is also produced for the housekeeper. When a guest arrives, a registration form is completed, the room number being added to the registration form from the arrivals list, and the form is placed in the customer file. If necessary any amendments to the booking dates are made to the reservations diary and the room chart. If a guest has no prior reservation, the diary and the room chart are used to check room availability and are then amended as required. The new guest details are added to the arrivals list.

Any room changes during the guest's stay are recorded on the registration form as well as the room chart.

While a guest is in the hotel, charges may be incurred in the bar/restaurant. In both cases, the guest is asked for name and room number and then signs the bar till slip or restaurant bill. The till/restaurant bills are passed to reception where they are filed, in room number order, in a box file calld 'chitties'.

Reservations also prepare a daily departure list for reception using the diary. Reception then prepares the guest bill using the customer file, (special rates may apply), standard tariff file, and the records of customer expenditure from the restaurant and bar. The room number is found from the registration form in the customer file and an undercopy of the bill is placed in this file. Private guests are required to settle their accounts on presentation of the bill. Company guests may, if they prefer, sign the bill as approved, in which case the top copy of the bill is passed to accounts (for presentation to the company). The departing guest's room number(s) is added to the departure list and passed to the housekeeper. A second copy of the guest bill goes to the accounts office.

Daily arrivals/departure lists and room lists are destroyed at the end of the day.

Examples of the forms used in the current booking and billing procedure are shown on the following pages.

Reservation Diary

Monday April 1st

Room Type	Details	Special Requirements
S	Bloggs, 15 The Fairway, Glos 0937 21759 Habitat Ltd	
S	Smith	
D(S)	Jones, 72 XYZ St., NW12 01 957 7246	
S) S)	Remshaw Ltd., Trading Est. Bolton 0235 91726	
T	Lawrence	

Number of Rooms

S ~~10~~ ~~9~~ 8 6
D ~~25~~ 24
T ~~10~~ 9
L 5

Tuesday April 2nd

Room Type	Details	Special Requirements
S	Bloggs	
T	Lawrence	
S	Lloyd, 95 The End, Chelt 0242 59321	Room 6
D	Williams, 19 Gt. Silver St., Harrogate 0329 63721	Vegetarian (both)

S ~~10~~ ~~9~~ 8
D ~~25~~ 24
T ~~10~~ 9
L 5 4 (Redecoration)

Appendix 1 Reservations Diary

Registration Form

Customer Name (Caps)   Company Name
_____   _____

Customer Address   Company Address
_____   _____

_____   _____

Date of   Car No.
Arrival   _____   _____
Date of   Number in
Departure   _____   Party   _____

Method of Payment
Cheque (sterling) / Travellers Cheque / Other:

How did they originally hear of us ?

Passport No   _____ Issued At   _____

Destination Address   _____

                       _____

                       _____

Room Number(s)   _____   Changed To   _____

                  _____   _____

                  _____   _____

Appendix 1 Registration Form

Room Chart

Date	G1 D	G2 D	F1 S	F2 T	F3 S	F4 S	
Monday 1st April		Bloggs	Smith	Lawrence	Renshaw	Renshaw	etc.
Tuesday 2nd April	Williams	↓	Lloyd	↓			

Appendix 1 Room Chart

Rooms List

ROOMS LIST FOR .... (date)

Guest Name	Room No.	New (✓)	Guest Name	Room No.	New (✓)

Appendix 1 Rooms List

Arrivals List

ARRIVALS FOR .... (date)

Guest Name	Room Type	Provisional/ Confirmed	Room No.	Date of Departure	Special Requirements

Appendix 1 Arrivals List

Standard Tariff List			
Double room per night	£	Double let as single	£
Twin room per night	£	Twin let as single	£
Single room per night	£		
Luxury room per night	£	Luxury let as single	£
Breakfast English	£		
Continental	£		
Table d'Hôte Lunch	£		
Table D'Hôte Dinner	£		
Tea	£		

Appendix 1 Standard Tariff List

Bar Chitty	
Bar	Date _____
Drinks	_____
	_____
	_____
	_____
Other	_____
	_____
	_____
Room Number	Guest Signature
_____	_____

Appendix 1 Bar Chitty

```
┌─────────────────────────────────────────────────┐
│              Restaurant Chitty                  │
├─────────────────────────────────────────────────┤
│  Restaurant  _____  Date  _____    │
│                                                 │
│  Breakfast    English          _____   │
│                                                 │
│               Continental      _____   │
│  Table d'Hôte  Lunch           _____   │
│  Table D'Hôte  Dinner          _____   │
│  Tea                           _____   │
│  Other                         _____   │
│                                _____   │
│                                _____   │
│                    Total       _____   │
│  Guest Signature                                │
│  _____   Room Number  _____     │
└─────────────────────────────────────────────────┘
```

Appendix 1 Restaurant Chitty

Departures List

DEPARTURES FOR .... (date)

Guest Name	Room No.	Guest Name	Room No.

Appendix 1 Departures List

Blacksands Hotel - Guest Account

Blacksands Hotel
Blacksands
Someshire

Tel: (0786) 513426

Date ....

Guest Name ....
Guest Address ....
....
....
.........................Post Code ....
Tel. No. ....

Company Name ....
Company Address ....
....
....
............................Post Code ....
Tel. No. ....

Accommodation

Date Arrival ....
Date Departure ....   No. Nights ....

Room Number ....   Room Type ....

Cost per Night £.................   Accommodation Total   ....

Restaurant

Restaurant Charges   ....

Bar

Bar Charges   ....

Other (Please Detail)
....
.... Total   ....

Total (excl. VAT)   ....

VAT   ....

Total   ....

Member of the Serve You Right Hotel Group

Appendix 1 Guest Account

Appendix 2 Stage 1 Products

The products for Stage 1 are all included in this appendix, the Current Services Description including the Data Flow Model, the Logical Data Model, Input/Output Descriptions and the Logical Data Flow Model.

The Requirements Catalogue has been put in Appendix 7. Although it is a product of Stage 1, the requirements are only started at this stage and are adjusted and changed throughout the system development cycle; therefore the catalogue has been allocated an appendix of its own.

Current Environment Data Flow Model

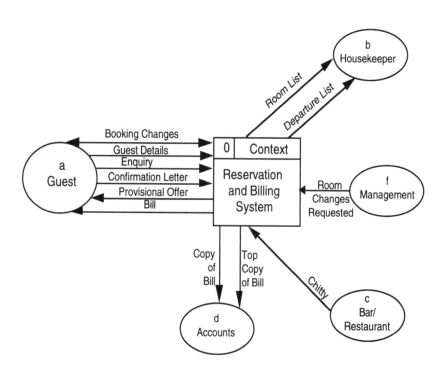

Appendix 2 Context Diagram Reservation and Billing System

External Entity Description   Page   of

SYSTEM: *Currrent - Hotel*	DATE / /	AUTHOR:

External Entity Id.	Name of External Entity	Description
a	*Guest*	*Customer having booking at hotel*
b	*Houskeeper*	*Housekeeper needs booking details for cleaning rota*
c	*Bar/Restaurant*	*Submit Chitties for Customer Expenditure in Restaurant and Bar*
d	*Accounts*	*Company Guest bills sent to Accounts Copies of settled bills sent to Accounts*
f	*Management*	*Hotel Management reserve the right to request room occupancy eg. for maintenance.*

Appendix 2 External Entity Description

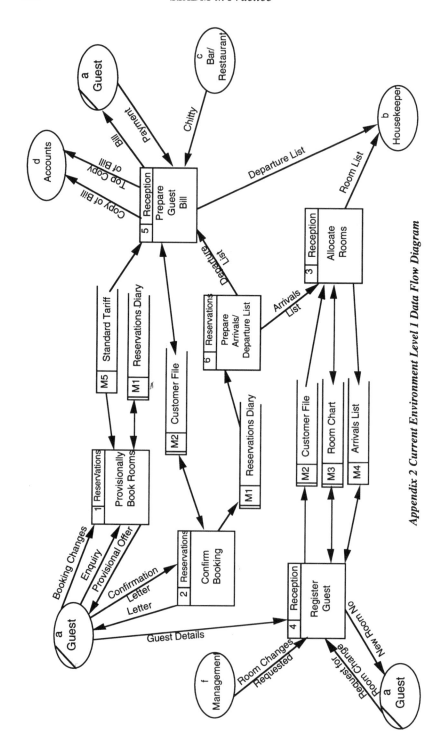

Appendix 2 Current Environment Level 1 Data Flow Diagram

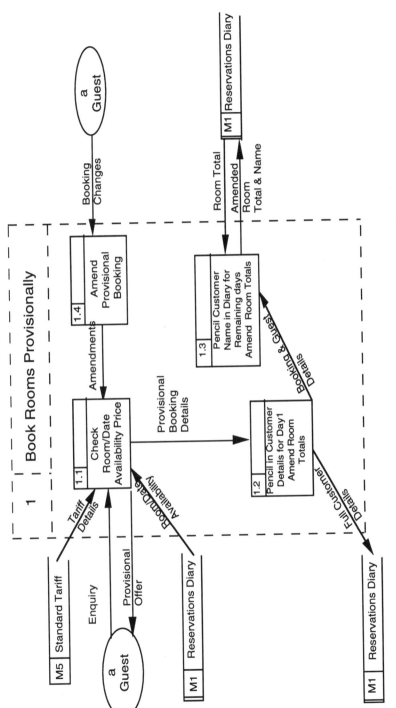

Appendix 2 Current Environment - Level 2 DFD Process 1

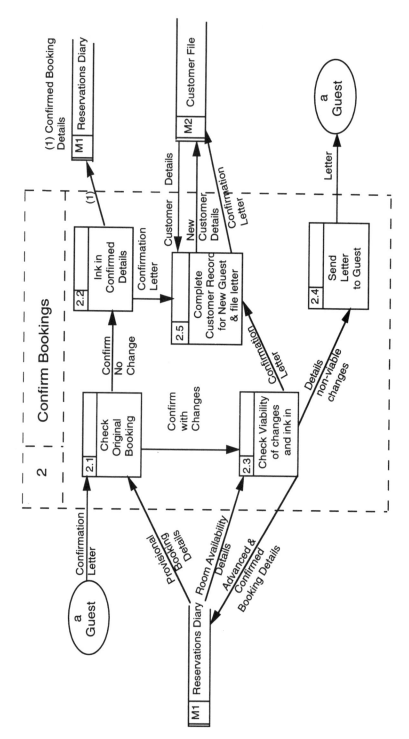

Appendix 2 Current Environment Level 2 DFD - Process 2

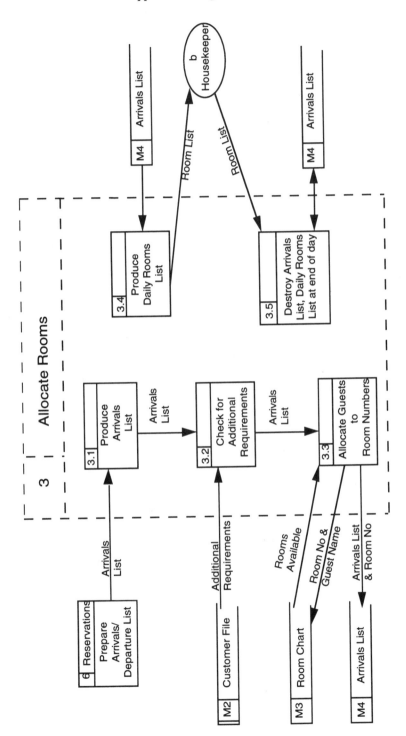

Appendix 2 Current Environment Level 2 DFD - Process 3

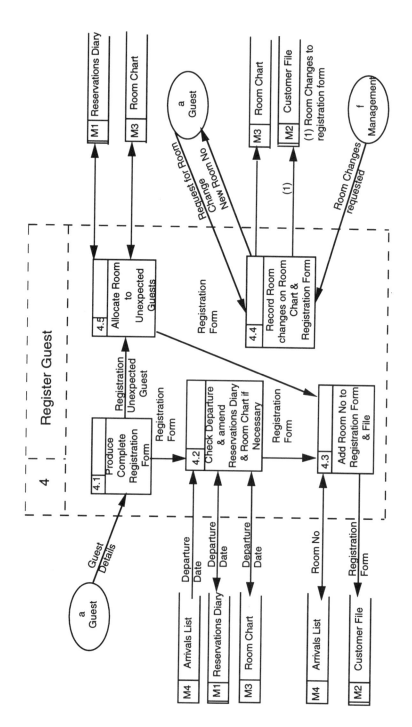

Appendix 2 Current Environment Level 2 DFD - Process 4

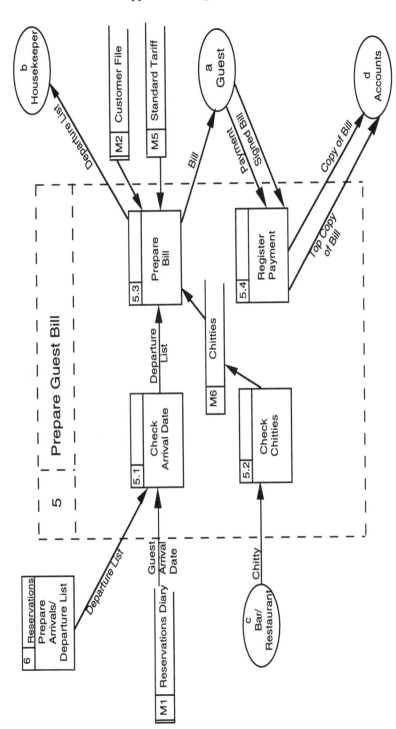

Appendix 2 Current Environment Level 2 DFD - Process 5

Elementary Process Description   Page   of

SYSTEM: *Currrent - Hotel*		DATE / /	AUTHOR:
Process ID	Process Name	Brief Description	

1.1	*Check Room/ Date Availability & Price*	*On receipt of Booking Enquiry*
		  - Check Reservations Diary for availability of room type
		       on required date
		  - Check Standard Tariff for Room Prices
		  - Make Provisional Booking Offer to Guest	

Appendix 2   Current Environment EPD - Process 1.1

Elementary Process Description   Page   of

SYSTEM: *Currrent - Hotel*	DATE / /	AUTHOR:

Process ID	Process Name	Brief Description
3.1	*Produce Arrivals List*	*Each morning -* - *Check Reservations Diary and put the name of each expected guest for that day on the arrivals list* - *Enter Room Type against each guest name*

Appendix 2 Current Environment - EPD Process 3.1

Elementary Process Description   Page   of

SYSTEM: *Currrent - Hotel*		DATE / /	AUTHOR:
Process ID	Process Name	Brief Description	

5.3	*Prepare Bill*	*For each entry on Departure List -*
		  - Check No of Days and Room Type
		  - Check Standard Tariff and Customer File for Room charge per day
		  - Calculate total room charge enter on Bill
		   - Check Chitties for Bar and Restaurant Charges
		  - Calculate Bar and restaurant charges and add to bill
		  - Add any other charges and total bill	

Appendix 2 Current Environment - EPD Process 5.3

Input/Output Description   Page 1 of

SYSTEM: *Currrent - Hotel*	DATE / /	AUTHOR:

~~Input /~~ Output		Name : *Guest Bill*

From	To	Data Flow Name	Data Content	Comment
Reception	*Guest*	*Bill*	*Customer Name*	
			No. Of Guests	
			Dates	
			Room No	

			Accommodation
			  Nights
			  No People
			  Price per night
			    Total Accommodation	

			Dinner
			  Meals
			  Price per Meal
			  No Meals
			    Total Meals	

			Drinks
			  Wine Chitties
			  Total Wine
			  Bar Chitties
			  Total Bar	

			Telephone Total	
			Other Total	
			Total Cost	
			Deposit	
			Total Due	

Appendix 2 Current Environment I/O Description - Guest Bill

Input/Output Description   Page 1 of

| SYSTEM: *Currrent - Hotel* | | DATE / / | | AUTHOR: |

| Input / ~~Output~~ | | Name :   *Bar Chitty* | | |

From	To	Data Flow Name	Data Content	Comment
Bar/Restaurant	*Reception*	*Chitty*	*Date*	
			Drinks	
			Other	
			Room No	
			Guest Signature	

Appendix 2 Current Environment I/O Description - Bar Chitty

Input/Output Description   Page 1 of

SYSTEM: *Currrent - Hotel*		DATE **/ /**	AUTHOR:

~~Input /~~ Output		Name : *Departure List*			
From	**To**	**Data Flow Name**	**Data Content**	**Comment**	
Reception	*Houskeeper*	*Departure List*	*Date* *Guest name* *Room No*		

Appendix 2   Current Environment I/O Description - Departure List

Input/Output Description   Page 1 of

SYSTEM: *Currrent - Hotel*		DATE / /	AUTHOR:

~~Input /~~ Output		Name : *Room List*	

From	To	Data Flow Name	Data Content	Comment
Reception	*Housekeeper*	*Room List*		
			Date	
			Guest name	
			Room No	

Appendix 2   Current Environment I/O Description - Room List

Current Environment Logical Data Model

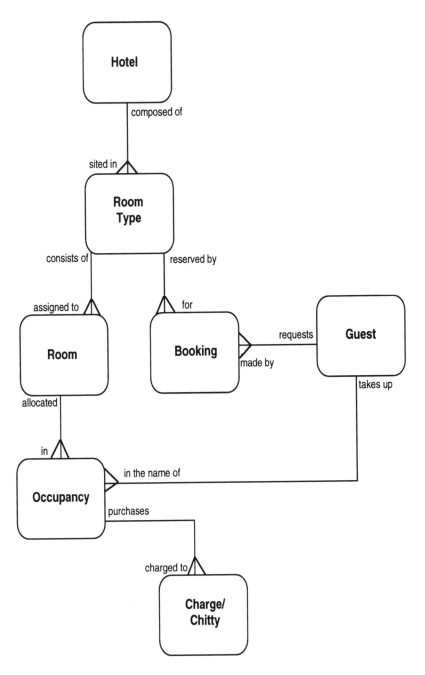

Appendix 2 Current Environment Logical Data Structure

Data Store/Entity X - Ref   Page   of

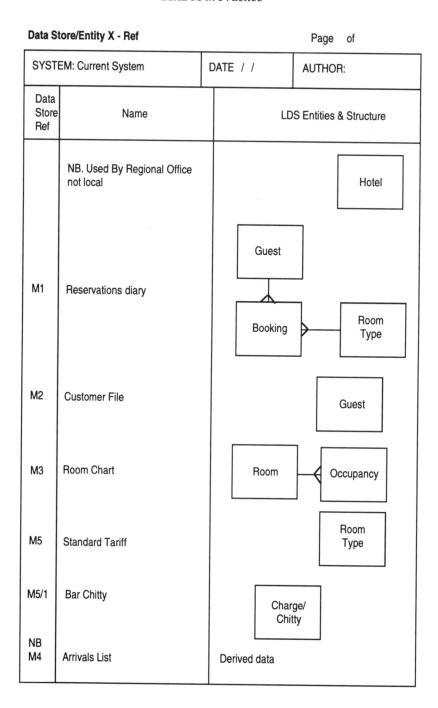

SYSTEM: Current System	DATE / /	AUTHOR:

Data Store Ref	Name	LDS Entities & Structure
	NB. Used By Regional Office not local	Hotel
M1	Reservations diary	Guest / Booking / Room Type
M2	Customer File	Guest
M3	Room Chart	Room / Occupancy
M5	Standard Tariff	Room Type
M5/1	Bar Chitty	Charge/ Chitty
NB M4	Arrivals List	Derived data

Appendix 2 Current Environment Data Store/Entity X-ref

Current Environment User Catalogue
User Catalogue   Page 1 of 2

SYSTEM: *Currrent - Hotel*	DATE / /	AUTHOR:

Name of User	Tasks	Data Stores Accessed
Reservations Clerk	Check availability of room	Reservations Diary
	Make provisional booking offer	Reservations Diary
	Enter booking details provisionally	Reservations Diary
	Note any special requirements	Reservations Diary Customer File
	Confirm Bookings	Reservations Diary
	Complete Customer Records	Reservations Diary
	Create Arrivals List	Reservations Diary Arrivals List
	Create Departures List	Reservation Diary Departures List

Appendix 2   Current Environment User Catalogue

User Catalogue   Page 2 of 2

SYSTEM: *Currrent - Hotel*	DATE / /	AUTHOR:

Name of User	Tasks	Data Stores Accessed
Receptionist	*Enter any Special requirements on Arrivals List*	*Reservations Diary Arrivals List*
	Allocate Room No	*Arrivals List Room Chart*
	Create Rooms List for Housekeeper	*Arrivals List*
	Complete Registration Form	*Customer File*
	Make any booking amendments	*Reservations Diary Customer File Room Chart*
	Complete all booking details for unexpected guests	*Reservations Diary Room Chart Customer File*
	Enter any Room changes on Registration Form and Room Chart	*Customer File Room Chart*
	Check Bar/Restaurant Chitties and file	*Chitties*
	Prepare Guest Bills	*Reservation Diary Customer File Chitties*
	Pass signed Top Copy of Bill to Accounts or Signed Copy Bill	
	Destroy Arrivals List, Departures List and Rooms List at end of day	*Arrivals List Departure List Room List*

Appendix 2   Current Environment User Catalogue

Current Environment Logical Data Flow Model

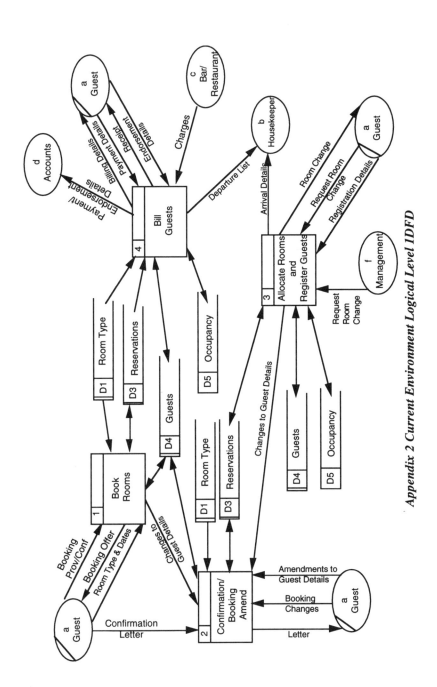

Appendix 2 Current Environment Logical Level 1 DFD

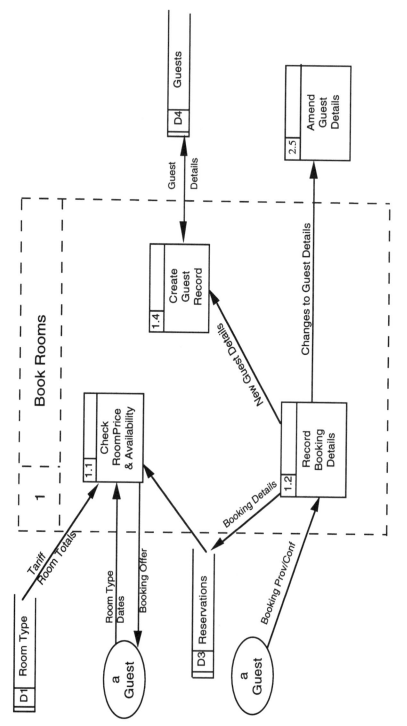

Appendix 2 Current Environment Logical Level 2 DFD - Process 1

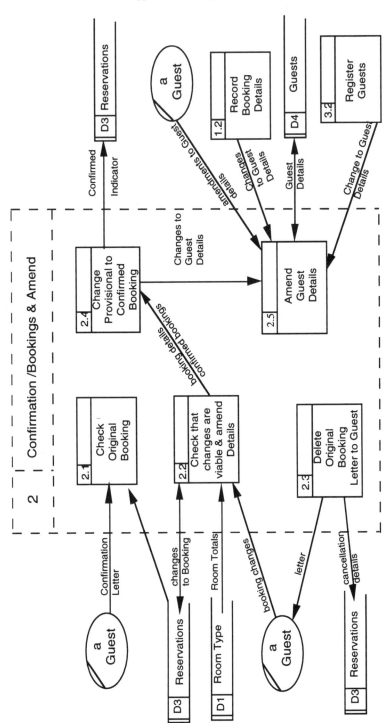

Appendix 2 Current Environment Logical Level 2 - Process 2

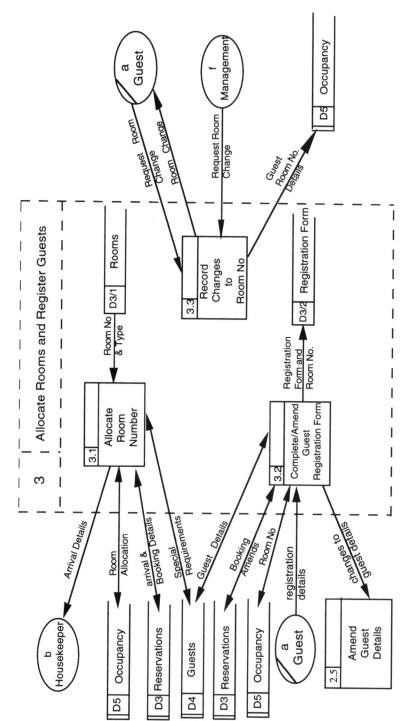

Appendix 2 Current Environment Logical Level 2 - Process 3

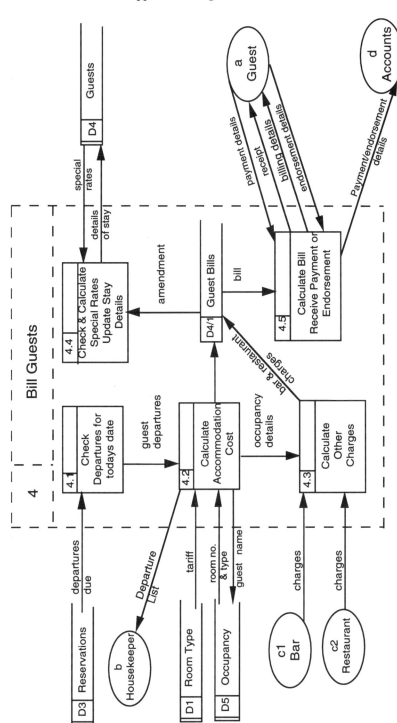

Appendix 2 Current Environment Logical Level 2- Process 4

Appendix 3 - Business System Option

Business System Option Overview Report

This option offers a computerised solution which includes automatic collection of data from the bar and restaurant.

The booking system will operate largely as at present although lost bookings or booking errors should almost be eliminated. Room allocation will be handled automatically by the system, although guests will still be able to request a particular room. An overbook function will be available to the hotel manager.

When the guest arrives, the system will generate a partially completed registration form for the guest to complete and an identification card for use by the guest during the stay.

When the guest incurs expenditure in the bar or restaurant which they wish to charge to their account, the identification card will be checked by a member of staff. (A machine readable strip could be easily introduced.) Point of sale terminals in the bar and restaurant will be used to record details of the charges and these charges files will be read at the time of billing. Bills will be produced quickly and automatically on a printer in Reception and errors in calculation or missing charges will be eliminated. Details of the bills and payments will be recorded to be passed on to Accounts.

The housekeeper may either be sent printouts of Arrivals and Departures or a terminal can be provided for enquiries by the housekeeper.

Management statistics can easily be provided on either a regular or an ad hoc basis.

Full back-up procedures will be available should there be any system failure.

Estimated Equipment Costs :

The cost for equipment outlined below apply to a stand-alone system for one hotel.

File Server and peripherals	20,000
Two Terminals (Reception)	1,500
One High Speed, High Quality Printer plus back-up printer	3,000
Four Point of Sale Terminals linked to File Server from Bar and Restaurant	8,000
System Software and Network	3,000
Application Software	15,000
	£50,500

Back-Up and maintenance of hardware to be negotiated with the supplier.

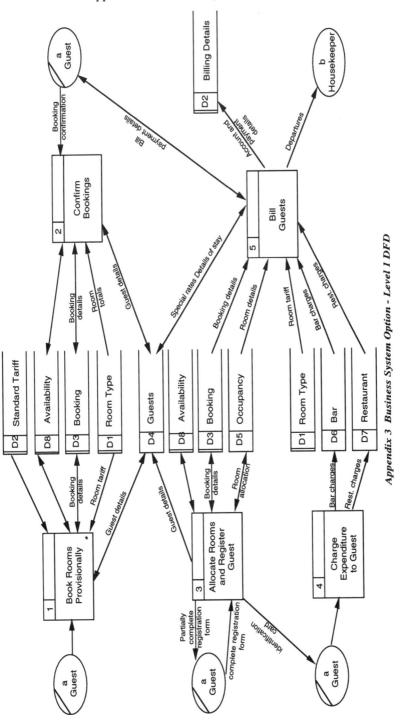

Appendix 3 Business System Option - Level 1 DFD

Implementation :

This would proceed on a hotel by hotel basis using one hotel in each region as a pilot and training site. It is expected that, initially, billing procedures would be implemented. Meanwhile a reservations system would be set up and fully implemented once the billing operation was working satisfactorily. Parallel running would be used for as short a period as possible.

Full staff training would be given.

Implications :

- Cost : £50,000 per hotel

- Disruption whilst changeover occurs

- Costs of training (time and expense)

- Impact on customers during changeover

- Reorganisation of reservations and reception staff so that the 'demarcation lines' are removed.

Advantages :

All the requirements in the Requirements Catalogue will be met. In particular, the accuracy of system data will be greatly enhanced and the bills will be produced more quickly. If a central booking system is introduced at a later date, this can easily be accommodated. Management information will be readily and easily available at any time.

Appendix 4 - Stage 3 Products

This appendix contains the requirements definition products of Stage 3, Data Flow Model, Logical Data Model, Entity/Event Model and the Function Decriptions.

Required Data Flow Model

This model starts on the following page.

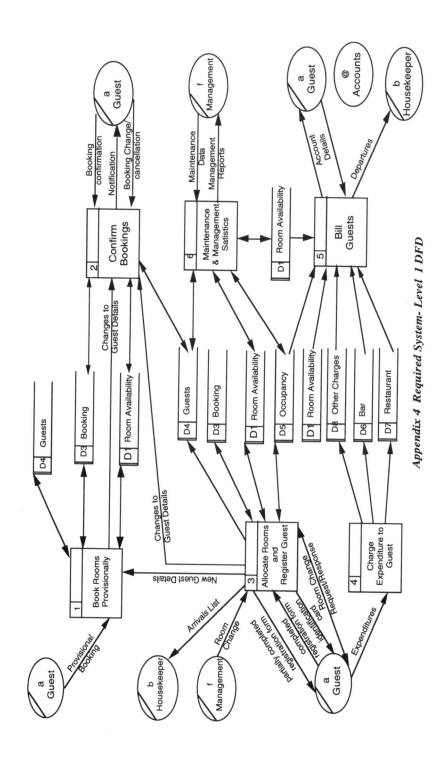

Appendix 4 Required System- Level 1 DFD

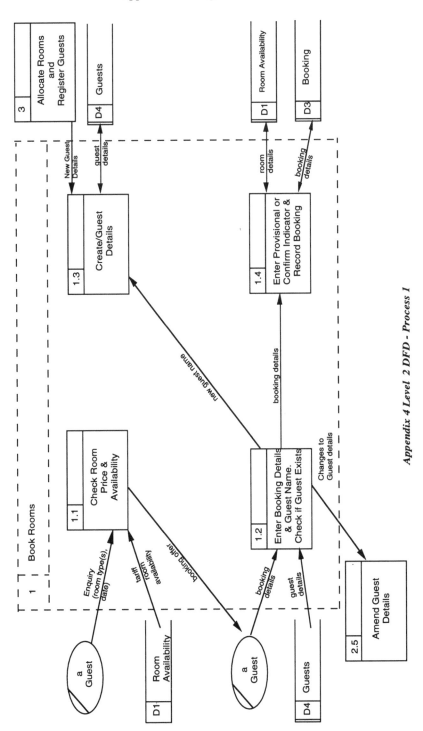

Appendix 4 Level 2 DFD - Process 1

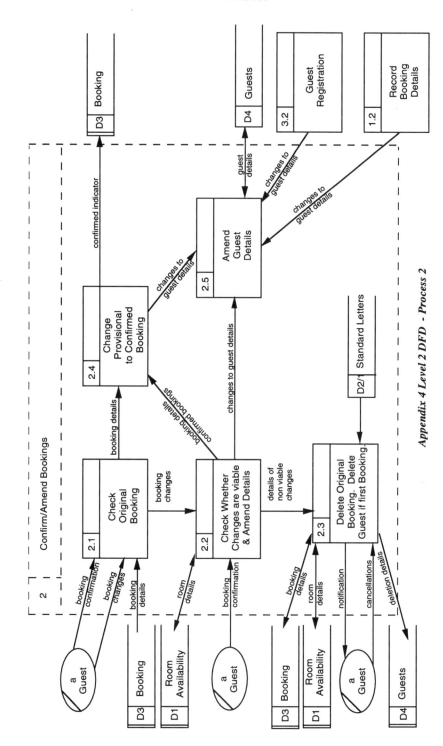

Appendix 4 Level 2 DFD - Process 2

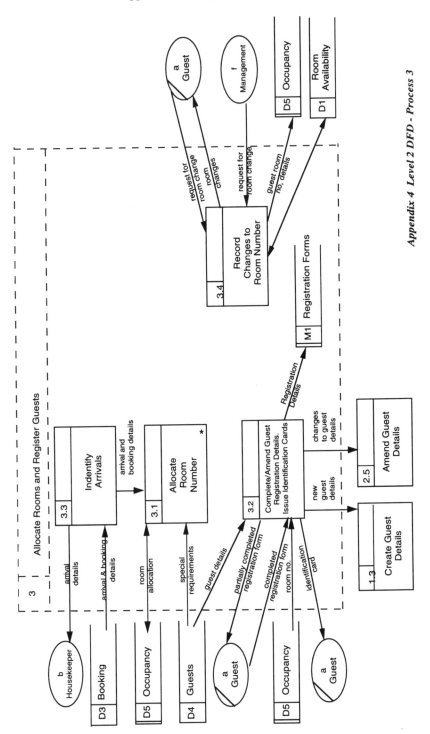

Appendix 4 Level 2 DFD - Process 3

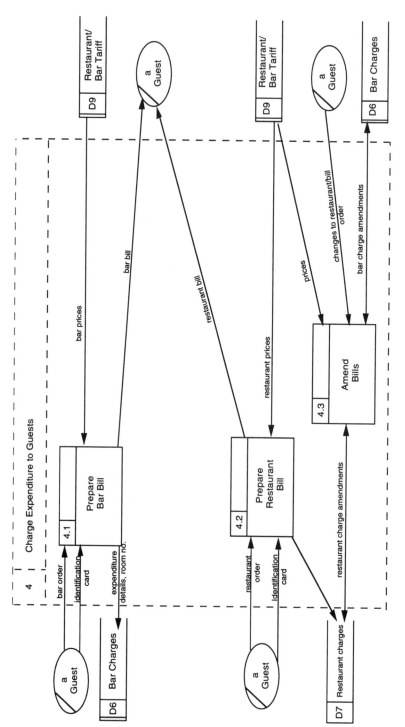

Appendix 4 Level 2 DFD - Process 4

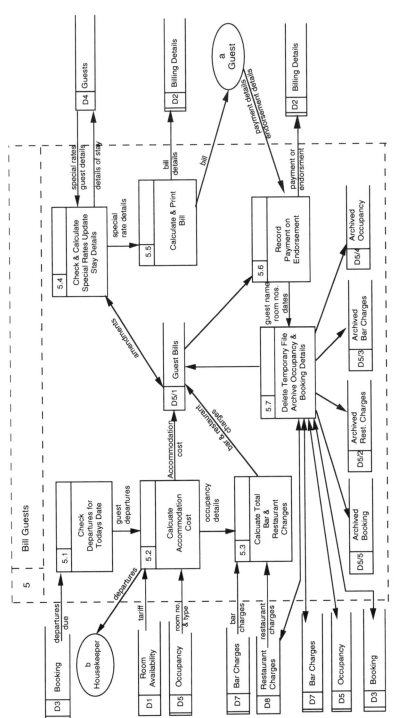

Appendix 4 Level 2 DFD - Process 5

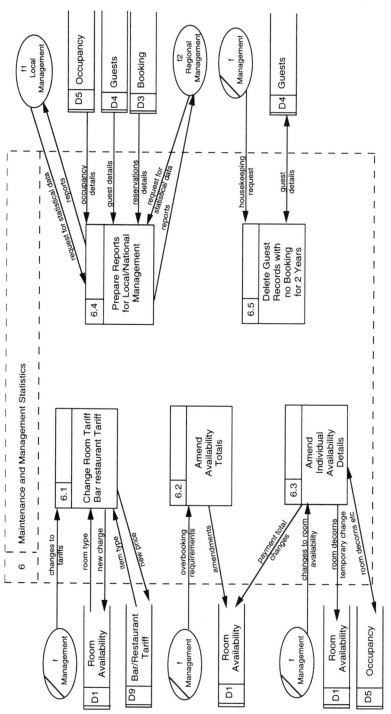

Appendix 4 Level 2 DFD - Process 6

Elementary Process Description   Page 1 of 1

SYSTEM: *Required - Hotel*	DATE / /	AUTHOR:

Process ID	Process Name	Brief Description
3.1	*Allocate Room*	*Read Booking to identify guests arriving, length of stay, room type, number of rooms required and any special requirements.* *Read Guests to check any permanent special requirements.* *Read Occupancy to identify room(s) of matching type which are vacant for the requested dates and allocate room numbers to the guest (under booker).* *(Algorithm to be supported for (1) and (2) taking account of bookings ahead)*

Appendix 4 Required System EPD - Process 3.1

Input/Output Description

SYSTEM: *Required - Hotel*	DATE / /	AUTHOR:

Input	Source: *Guest*	Recipient : *Hotel*	Data Flow Name :	*Provisional Booking*
~~Output~~				

Data Item	Comments
Guest Surname	
Guest Forename	
Guest Address	
Guest Tel No.	
Room Type	
No. Rooms	
No. Guests	
Date of Arrival	
Date of Departure	

Appendix 4 Required System Input/Ouptut Description - Provisional Booking

Input/Output Description Page 2 of 11

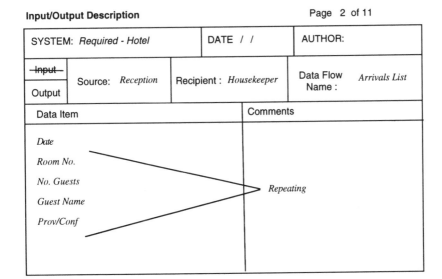

Appendix 4 Input/Output Description - Arrivals List

Input/Output Description Page 3 of 11

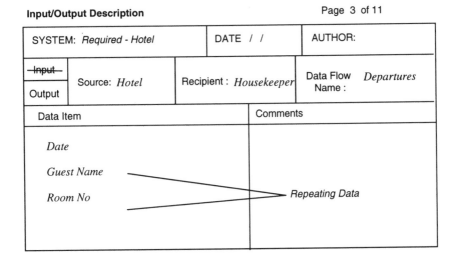

Appendix 4 Input/Output Description - Departure List

Input/Output Description   Page 4 of 11

SYSTEM: *Required - Hotel*	DATE / /	AUTHOR:

~~Input~~ Output	Source: *Hotel*	Recipient : *Guest*	Data Flow Name : *Identification Card*

Data Item	Comments
Guest Surname *Guest Forename* *Room No.*	

Appendix 4 Input/Output Description - Identification Card

Input/Output Description   Page 6 of 11

SYSTEM: *Required - Hotel*	DATE / /	AUTHOR:

Input ~~Output~~	Source: *Management*	Recipient : *Hotel*	Data Flow Name : *Overbooking Requirement*

Data Item	Comments
Room Type *Room No.* *Percentage Overbook*	*Repeating*

Appendix 4 Input/Output Description - Overbooking Requirement

Input/Output Description   Page 5 of 11

SYSTEM: *Required - Hotel*	DATE / /	AUTHOR:

Input	Source: *Guest*	Recipient : *Reception*	Data Flow Name : *Completed Registration*
~~Output~~			

Data Item	Comments
Guest Surname	
Guest Forename	
Guest Address	
Guest Tel No.	
Company Name	
Company Address	
Car Reg.	
No. Guests	
Date of Arrival	
Date of Departure	
Method of Payment	(Cheque,Sterling,Credit Card, Account)
Passport No.	
Issued By	
Destination Address	
Room No(s)	Repeating

Appendix 4 Required System Input/Output Description - Completed Registration

174   *SSADM in Practice*

Input/Output Description   Page 7 of 11

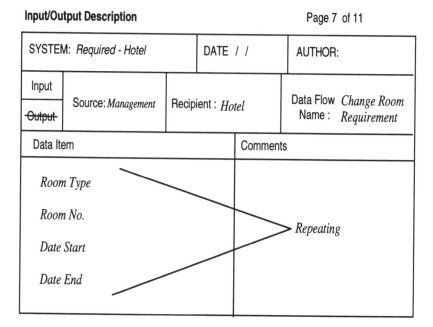

SYSTEM: *Required - Hotel*	DATE / /	AUTHOR:
Input ~~Output~~ Source: *Management*	Recipient : *Hotel*	Data Flow *Change Room* Name : *Requirement*
Data Item		Comments
Room Type *Room No.* *Date Start* *Date End*		*Repeating*

Appendix 4 Required System Input/Output Description - Change Room
Requirement

Input/Output Description   Page 8 of 11

SYSTEM: *Required - Hotel*	DATE / /	AUTHOR:
Input ~~Output~~ Source: *Management*	Recipient : *Hotel*	Data Flow *Archiving* Name : *Request*
Data Item		Comments
Date		*Date for two year calculation*

Appendix 4 Required System Input/Output Description - Archiving
Request

Input/Output Description

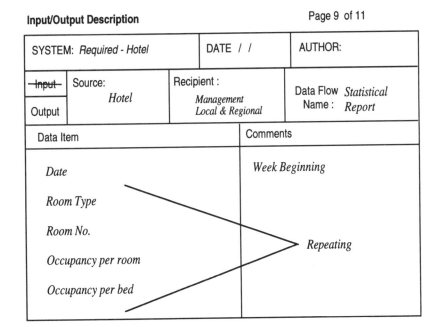

SYSTEM: *Required - Hotel*	DATE / /	AUTHOR:
~~Input~~ / Output	Source: *Hotel*	Recipient : *Management Local & Regional*	Data Flow Name : *Statistical Report*

Data Item	Comments
Date	*Week Beginning*
Room Type	
Room No.	
Occupancy per room	*Repeating*
Occupancy per bed	

Appendix 4 Required System Input/Output Description - Statistical Report

Input/Output Description   Page 10 of 11

SYSTEM: *Required - Hotel*	DATE / /	AUTHOR:

~~Input~~ Output	Source: *Hotel*	Recipient : *Guest*	Data Flow Name : *Account Details*

Data Item	Comments
Guest Surname	
Guest Forename	
No. Guests	
Date of Arrival	
Date of Departure	
Method of Payment	
Room No(s)	
Cost per Night	
Accommodation Total	
No. Meals	
Total Cost of Meals	
Total Restaurant Costs	
Total Bar Costs	
Total Telephone Costs	
Other	
Total Cost	
Less Discount	
Less Deposit	
Total Due	
Vat Reg No	

Appendix 4 Required System Input/Output Description - Account Details

Input/Output Description

SYSTEM: *Required - Hotel*	DATE / /	AUTHOR:

| Input | Source: | Recipient : | Data Flow | *Changes to* |
| ~~Output~~ | *Management* | *Hotel* | Name : | *Tariff* |

Data Item	Comments

Room Type

Cost Per Night

Single Supplement

Repeating

Breakfast English Price

Breakfast Continental Price

Table d'Hôte Lunch Price

Table d' Hôte Dinner Price

Tea

Item Bar Stock

Price Bar Stock

Repeating

Appendix 4 Required System Input/Output Description - Changes to Tariff

Logical Data Model

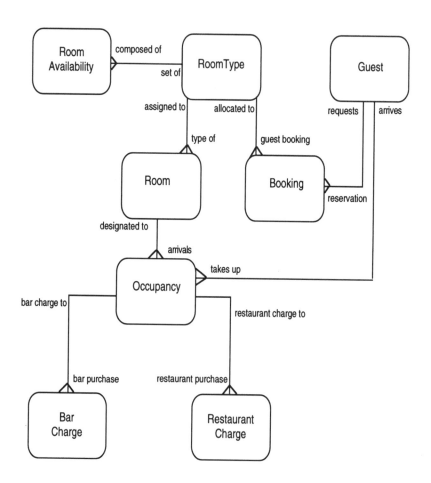

Appendix 4 Logical Data Structure (Required System)

Data Store/Entity X - Ref Page 1 of 1

SYSTEM: Required System	DATE / /	AUTHOR:

Data Store Ref	Name	LDS Entities & Structure
D1	Room tariff & totals	Room Type
D3	Reservations	Booking
D4	Guests	Guest
D5	Occupancy	Occupancy >— Room
D6	Bar	Bar Charge
D7	Restaurant	Restaurant Charge
D8	Room Availability	Room Availability
NB D2	Billing details -	Output Report

Appendix 4 Data Store / Entity Cross Reference (Required System)

User Role	Activities
Reservations	Make Provisional Booking Confirm Booking Change Booking Cancel Booking Amend Guest Details
Reception	Room Allocation Amend Allocation Guest Registration Arrivals List Raise Guest Bill Amend Guest Bill Amend Guest Details
Local Management	Amend Tariffs Amend Availability Delete Guests Request Reports
Regional Management	Request Reports
Bar Cashier	Charge Expenditure
Restaurant Cashier	Charge Expenditure

Functions / Roles	Booking	Allocation	Registration	Acounting	Maintenance
Reservations	*				
Reception		*	*	*	
Local Management					*
Regional Management					*
Bar Cashier				*	
Restaurant Cashier				*	

Appendix 4 User Roles and Function Matrix

Entity Descriptions Required System

Entity Description - Part One		
System : Hotel	**Variant :** Required	
Entity Name : Bar Charge	**Entity ID :** D6	
Attribute Name	**Primary Key**	**Foreign Key**
Room No	*	
Date		
Time		
Details		
Total Cost		

Relationship No.	'must be'/ 'may be'	'Either' / 'or'	Link Phrase	'one & only one'/'one or more'	Object Entity Name
13	must be		held by	one and only one	Occupancy

Entity Description - Part Two

System : *Hotel*	Variant : *Required*

Entity Name :   *Bar Charge*

User Role	Access Rights
Bar Cashier	*Read, Write*
Reception	*Read, Write*

Owner :

Growth Period :
  A set of Bar Charge will grow over an occupancy period

Additional Relationships :

Archive and Destruction :
        archive - on departure of guest
        delete - on departure of guest

Security Measures :
        Only management can alter tariff

State Indicator Values :
      1 - created   2 - Amend or Delete

Notes :

Entity Description - Part One

System :	Hotel	Variant :	Required
Entity Name :	Booking	**Entity ID :**	D3

Attribute Name	Primary Key	Foreign Key
Guest Surname	*	
Guest Forename	*	
Date Arrival	*	
Date Depart		
Room Type		
No Of Rooms		
Provisional/Confirmed		
Special Requirements		

Relationship No.	'must be'/ 'may be'	'Either' / 'or'	Link Phrase	'one & only one'/'one or more'	Object Entity Name
2	must be		held by	one and only one	Guest
3	must be		linked to	one and only one	Room Type

Entity Description - Part Two

System : *Hotel*	Variant : *Required*

Entity Name :   *Booking*

User Role	Access Rights
Reservations	*Create, Read, Update, Delete*
Reception	
Management	*Read, Update, Delete*
	Read

Owner :

Growth Period :
   One Year

Additional Relationships :

Archive and Destruction :
   Archive 'Guest Departs'
   Delete - 'Cancel Booking'

Security Measures :

State Indicator Values :
   1 - provisional   2 - new confirmed
   3 - Arrival (no booking) 4 - old confirmed

Notes :

Entity Description - Part One

System : Hotel	Variant : Required

Entity Name : Guest	Entity ID : D4

Attribute Name	Primary Key	Foreign Key
Guest Surname	*	
Guest Forename		
Guest Address		
Company		
Special Requirements		
Date of Last Stay		
Special Discount		

Relationship No.	'must be'/ 'may be'	'Either' / 'or'	Link Phrase	'one & only one'/'one or more'	Object Entity Name
1	may be		linked to	one or more	Booking

Entity Description - Part Two

System : *Hotel*	Variant : *Required*

Entity Name : *Guest*

User Role	Access Rights
Reservations	*Create, Read, Write*
Reception	*Create, Read, Write*
Management	*Read, Delete*

Owner :

Growth Period :
A two year growth period

Additional Relationships :

Archive and Destruction :
delete - no booking for two years

Security Measures :

State Indicator Values :
1,2,3 - created   1-4 - Amend or Delete

Notes :

Entity Description - Part One

System :	Hotel	Variant :	Required

Entity Name :	Occupancy	Entity ID :	D5

Attribute Name	Primary Key	Foreign Key
Room No	*	
Date		
Guest Surname		
Guest Forename		
Code (B(ooking), O(ther))		

Relationship No.	'must be'/ 'may be'	'Either' / 'or'	Link Phrase	'one & only one'/'one or more'	Object Entity Name
10	must be		linked to	one and only one	Room
11	may be		linked to	zero or many	Bar Charge
12	may be		linked to	zero or many	Restaurant Charge

Entity Description - Part Two

System : *Hotel*	Variant : *Required*

Entity Name : *Occupancy*

User Role	Access Rights
Reception	*Create, Read, Write*
Management	*Create, Read, Write*

Owner :

Growth Period :
A set of occupancy occurrence live only for duration of booking

Additional Relationships :

Archive and Destruction :
Delete - guest departs

Security Measures :

State Indicator Values :
1,2 - created   3 - Amend   1-3 Delete

Notes :

Entity Description - Part One			
System : *Hotel*		**Variant :** *Required*	
Entity Name : *Restaurant Charge*		**Entity ID :** *D7*	
Attribute Name		**Primary Key**	**Foreign Key**
Room No		*	
Date			
Meal Type (B,C,L,T,D,S)			
Details			
Total Cost			

Relationship No.	'must be'/ 'may be'	'Either' / 'or'	Link Phrase	'one & only one'/'one or more'	Object Entity Name
14	*must be*		*held by*	*one and only one*	*Occupancy*

Entity Description - Part Two

System : *Hotel*

Variant : *Required*

Entity Name :   *Restaurant Charge*

User Role	Access Rights
RestaurantCashier	*Read, Write*
Reception	*Read, Write*

Owner :

Growth Period :
   A set of Restaurant Charge will grow over an occupancy period

Additional Relationships :

Archive and Destruction :
     archive - on departure of guest
     delete - on departure of guest

Security Measures :
     Only management can alter tariff

State Indicator Values :
    1 - created   2 - Amend or Delete

Notes :

Entity Description - Part One					
System : Hotel			**Variant :** Required		
Entity Name : Room Availability			**Entity ID :** D1		
Attribute Name			**Primary Key**	**Foreign Key**	
Room Type			*		
Date					
Total Available					

Relationship No.	'must be'/ 'may be'	'Either' / 'or'	Link Phrase	'one & only one'/'one or more'	Object Entity Name
6	must be		linked to	one and only one	Room Type

Entity Description - Part Two

System : *Hotel*	Variant : *Required*

Entity Name :   *Room Availability*

User Role	Access Rights
Reservations	*Create, Read, Update, Delete*
Reception	
Management	*Read, Update*
	Read

Owner :

Growth Period :
Covers one year period, occurrences for day deleted at day end and new occurrences (365 days ahead) created at day start. (no expected growth)

Additional Relationships :

Archive and Destruction :
Archive 'Day End'
Delete - 'Day End'

Security Measures :

State Indicator Values :
1 - created   2 - amended

Notes :

Entity Description - Part One

System : *Hotel*	**Variant :** *Required*
Entity Name : *Room Type*	**Entity ID :**

Attribute Name	Primary Key	Foreign Key
Room Type	*	
Tariff		
Total Available		
Overbook %		

Relationship No.	'must be'/ 'may be'	'Either' / 'or'	Link Phrase	'one & only one'/'one or more'	Object Entity Name
4	*may be*		*held by*	*one or more*	*Booking*
5	*may be*		*held by*	*one or more*	*Daily Availability*
7	*must be*		*held by*	*one or more*	*Room*

Entity Description - Part Two

System : *Hotel*	Variant : *Required*

Entity Name : *Room Type*

User Role	Access Rights
Reservations	*Read*
Reception	*Read*
Management	*Create, Read, Delete*

Owner :

Growth Period :
No growth expected, unless new room types are structured

Additional Relationships :

Archive and Destruction :
      archive - if changes made to occurrences
      delete - only if structural alterations remove a type

Security Measures :
      Only management can alter tariff and overbook

State Indicator Values :
     1 - created   2 - amended tariff   3 - amended overbook

Notes :

Entity Description - Part One					
System : Hotel			**Variant :** Required		
Entity Name : Room			**Entity ID :**		
Attribute Name			**Primary Key**		**Foreign Key**
Room Type			*		
Room No					
Facilities					
Relationship No.	**'must be'/ 'may be'**	**'Either' / 'or'**	**Link Phrase**	**'one & only one'/'one or more'**	**Object Entity Name**
8	must be		linked to	one and only one	Room Type
9	must be		held by	one and only one	Occupancy

Entity Description - Part Two

System : *Hotel*	Variant : *Required*

Entity Name : *Room*

User Role	Access Rights
Management	*Create, Read, Write, Delete*

Owner :

Growth Period :
  No growth expected, unless structural changes made to fabric of hotel

Additional Relationships :

Archive and Destruction :
  archive - if changes made to occurrences
  delete - if a room is taken out of commission

Security Measures :
  Only management can access this entity directly

State Indicator Values :
  1 - created   2 - amended type   3 - amended facilities

Notes :

Function Definitions

Function Definition	Function Name : *Booking*	ID : *1*

User Roles :   *Reservation Clerk*

Function Description :
On receipt of a booking enquiry, dates, room type and number of guests are checked in Room Availability, if available a booking offer is made. If the booking offer is accepted guest and booking details are recorded as a provisional or confirmed booking. On receipt of confirmation the confirm indicator is set. If changes to the booking are requested, availability is checked as for enquiry. If the changes are viable the booking details are changed and the confirmed indicator set. If not, the booking is cancelled and a letter sent to the guest. Guest details can be amended during the booking procedure.

Error Handling :

DFD Processes :
1.1,1.2,1.4,2.1,2.2,2.3,2.4,2.5

Events (Frequency) :
Booking Enquiry, New Provisional Booking, New Confirmed Booking, Confirmed Booking, Booking Change, Booking Cancelled, Amend Guest Details

I/O Descriptions :
Booking Enquiry, Booking Offer, Booking Confirmation, Booking Changes, Notification, Cancellation, Amendment of Guest Details

I/O Structures :
Booking Enquiry, Provisional Booking, Confirmed Booking, Changed Booking

Requirements Catalogue Refs :

Volumes :

Related Functions :
Registration, Allocation, Raise Guest Bills, Maintenance

Enquiries (Frequency)

Common Processing :

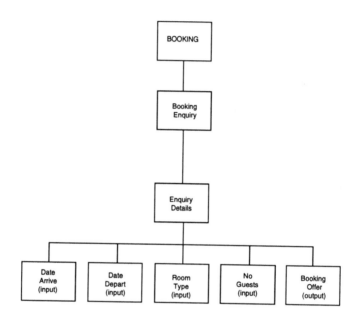

Appendix 4 Input/Output Structure - Booking Enquiry

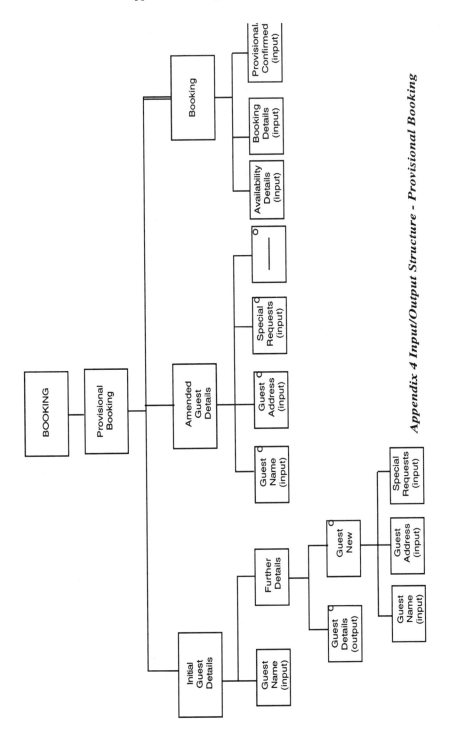

Appendix 4 Input/Output Structure - Provisional Booking

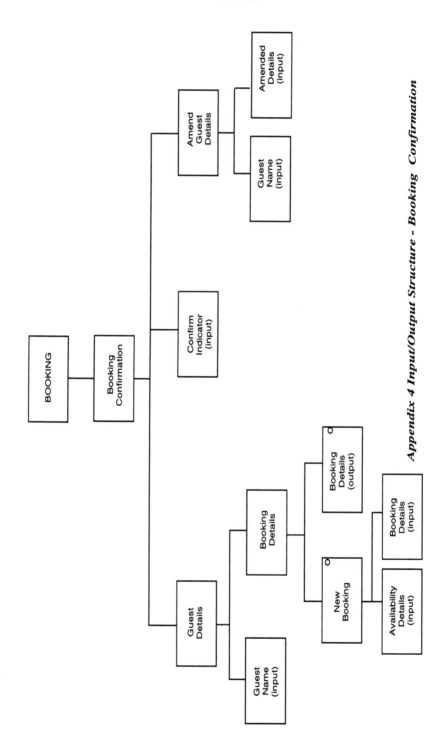

Appendix 4 Input/Output Structure - Booking Confirmation

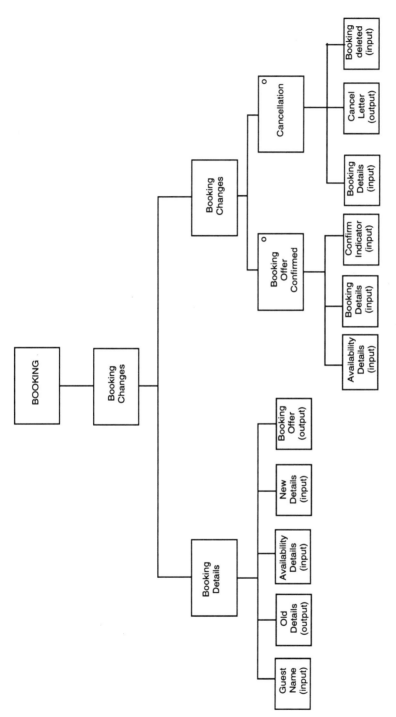

Appendix 4 Input/Output Structure Booking Changes

Function Definition	**Function Name :** *Room Allocation*	**ID :** *2*

User Roles :   *Receptionist*

Function Description :
Allocation is an automatic process carried out each morning (daily). The booking arrivals for the day are checked and allocated to the correct room type available for the duration of the stay, special requests for rooms are checked , the allocation is stored in Occupancy, and an arrivals list is passed to the housekeeper.

Error Handling :

DFD Processes :
3.3, 3.1, 3.4

Events (Frequency) :
Allocation of room, change of room, arrival list creation

I/O Descriptions :
Arrival Details, Request Room Changes, Room Changes

I/O Structures :
Allocation

Requirements Catalogue Refs :

Volumes :

Related Functions :
Booking, Maintenance

Enquiries (Frequency)

Common Processing :

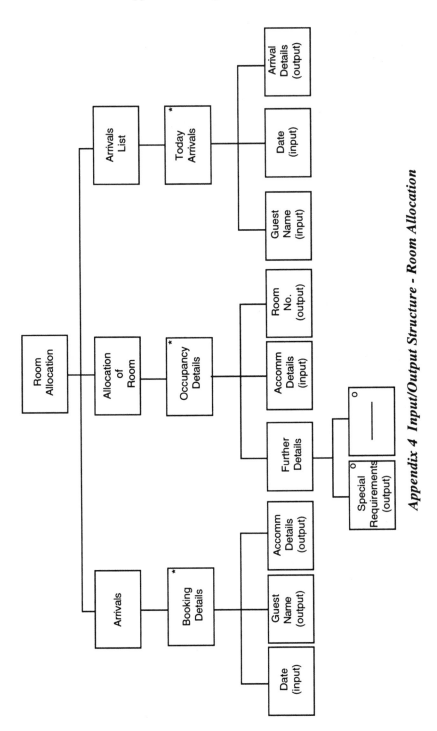

Appendix 4 Input/Output Structure - Room Allocation

Function Definition	**Function Name :** *Charge Expenditure*	**ID :** *3*

User Roles :   *Receptionist, Bar Cashier, Restaurant Cashier*

Function Description :
Expenditure in the Bar and Restaurant is entered into a POS terminal with Room Number, Date and Time, reference is made to the Bar/Restaurant Tariff file for prices, the details are then written to the respective Charge File.
Changes to the Charge Files are made when necessary at reception when the amendment is entered with Room Number, Time and Date into the charge file.

Error Handling :

DFD Processes :
4.1,4.2,4.3

Events (Frequency) :
Charge Bar Expenditure, Charge Restaurant Expenditure, Amend Expenditure

I/O Descriptions :
Identification Card, Amendments, Restaurant Order, Bar Order

I/O Structures :
Charge Expenditure

Requirements Catalogue Refs :

Volumes :

Related Functions :
Maintenance, Raise Guest Bill

Enquiries (Frequency)

Common Processing :

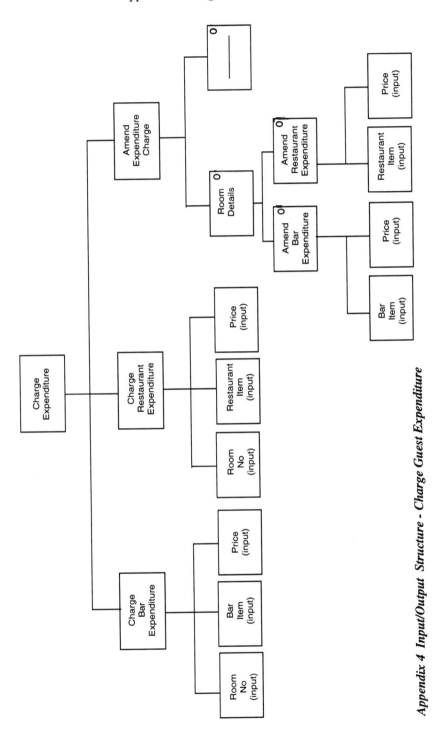

Appendix 4 Input/Output Structure - Charge Guest Expenditure

Function Definition	**Function Name :** *Guest Registration*	**ID :** *4*

User Roles :   *Receptionist*

Function Description :
On arrival of a guest a partially completed Registration Form is printed, this is completed by the guest. An identification card is produced to be used by the guest to authorise expenditure.

Error Handling :

DFD Processes :
3.2

Events (Frequency) :
Arrival of Guest

I/O Descriptions :
Identification Card, Registration Details

I/O Structures :
Registration of Guest

Requirements Catalogue Refs :

Volumes :

Related Functions :
Booking

Enquiries (Frequency)

Common Processing :

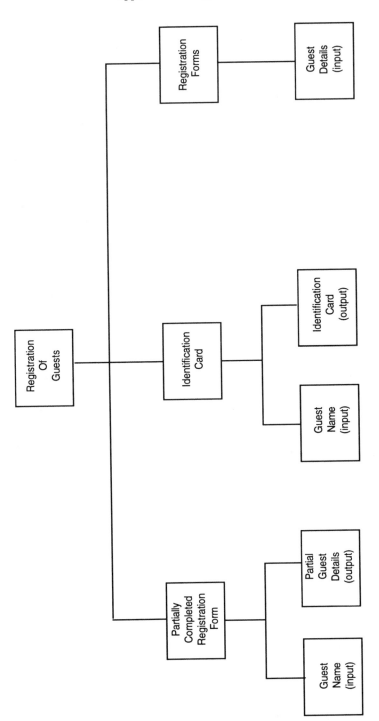

Appendix 4 Input/Output Structure - Registration of Guests

Function Definition	**Function Name :** *Maintenance*	**ID :** 5

User Roles :   *Local Management, Regional Management*

Function Description :
*Requests from Local and regional management will be serviced through this
function. Updating the Standard Tariff Details, and overbooking levels.
Management booking of rooms for events, decoration and finally deletion of old
guest details (No booking for 2 years)*

Error Handling :

DFD Processes :
6.1, 6.2, 6.3, 6.5

Events (Frequency) :
*No booking for 2 years, Room Decoration, Price Change, Availability Change, Structural
alterations.*

I/O Descriptions :
*Changes to tariffs, overbooking requirements, changes to room availability, housekeeping
request, structural alterations*

I/O Structures :
Maintenance, Changes to Tariff

Requirements Catalogue Refs :

Volumes :

Related Functions :
Booking

Enquiries (Frequency)

Common Processing :

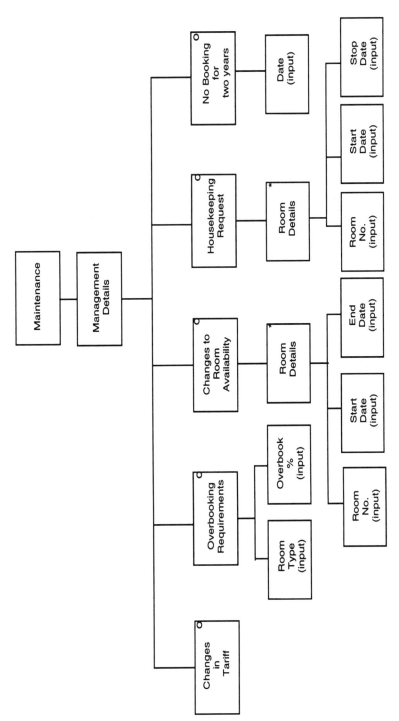

Appendix 4 Input/Output Structure - Maintenance

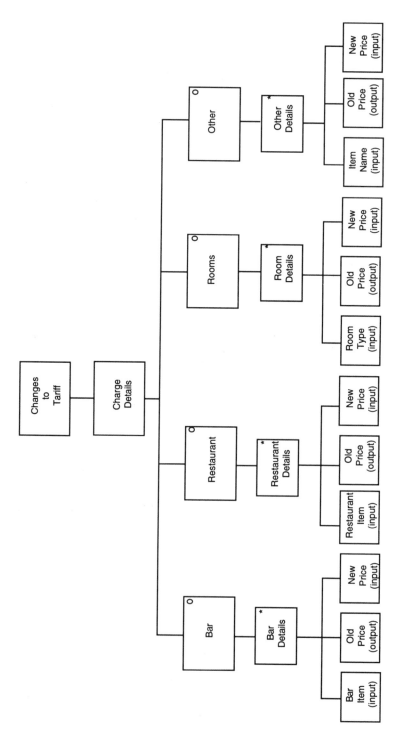

Appendix 4 Input/Output Structure - Changes to Tariff

Function Definition	**Function Name :** *Statistical Reports*	**ID :** 6

User Roles : *Local Management, Regional Management*

Function Description :
Statistical report generation on occupancy, bookings and guests.

Error Handling :

DFD Processes :
6.5

Events (Frequency) :
Request Reports

I/O Descriptions :
Request for reports

I/O Structures :
Statistical Reports

Requirements Catalogue Refs :

Volumes :

Related Functions :
Booking

Enquiries (Frequency)

Common Processing :

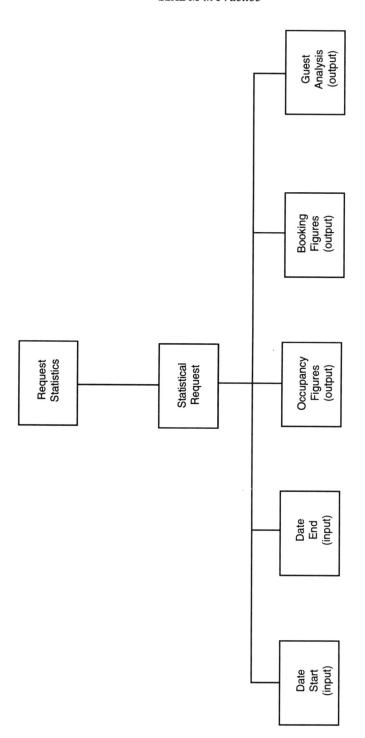

Appendix 4 Input/Output Structure - Request Statistics

Function Definition	Function Name : *Raise Guest Bill*	ID : 7

User Roles :   *Receptionist*

Function Description :
An automatic process is invoked at the start of the day to check for guests departing; the guest name is added to a departure list. Occupancy is then checked for accommodation details, the room number is added to the departure list and accommodation cost calculated. A copy of the departure list is passed to the housekeeper.
At the time of guest departure, expenditure in the Bar and Restaurant are calculated and added to the bill details. Special Rates are checked in the Guest file and added to bill details if applicable, full guest details are also obtained and added to the file. The final totals are then calculated and the bill printed.
At day end the Bar, Restaurant ,Occupancy and Booking details are archived and the Temporary Guest Bills deleted.

Error Handling :

DFD Processes :
   6.5

Events (Frequency) :
   Guest Departs

I/O Descriptions :
   Departures Due, Account Details

I/O Structures :
   Guest Departure, Guest Accounts, Departures Due

Requirements Catalogue Refs :

Volumes :

Related Functions :
   Booking

Enquiries (Frequency)

Common Processing :

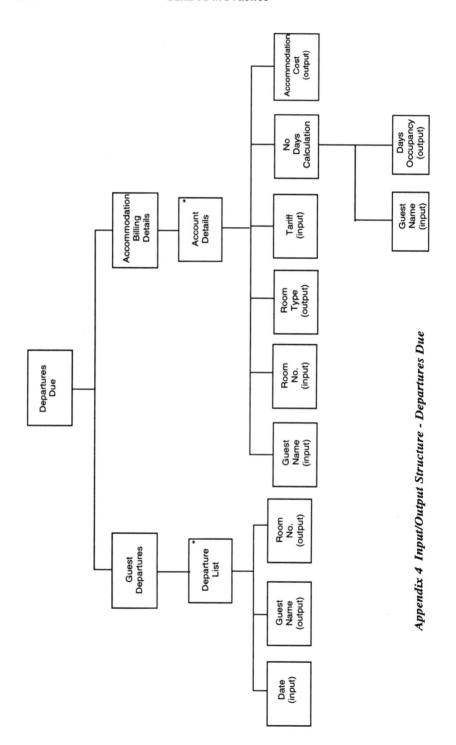

Appendix 4 Input/Output Structure - Departures Due

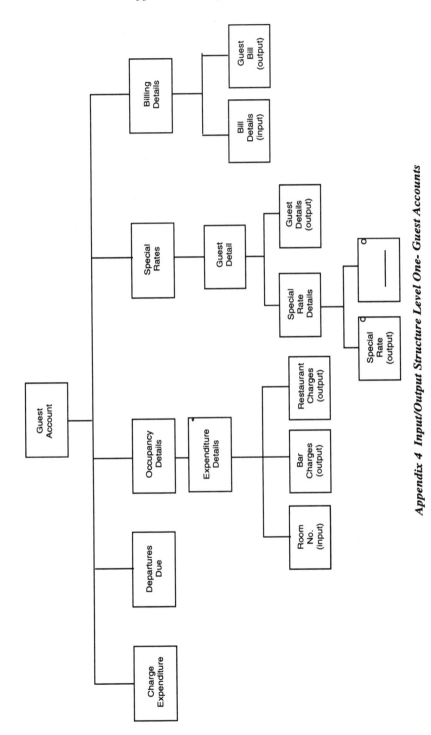

Appendix 4 Input/Output Structure Level One- Guest Accounts

Entity/Event Model

MATRIX

| SYSTEM: Reservations & Billing | | | | | | | DATE / / | AUTHOR: |

Event	Guest	Booking	Occupancy	Bar Charge	Restaurant Charge	Room Avail.	Room	Room Type
Provisional booking	I	I				M		
Confirmed booking	I/M	M				M		
Guest arrival(no Booking)	M/I	I	I			M		
Change Booking	M	M	M					
Cancel Booking	M/D	D	D			M		
Non-Arrival		D	D			M		
Guest Depart	M	D	D	D	D			
Room Allocated			I					
Decoration			M			M		
Room Change			M			M		
Decoration Complete			D			M		
Guest Registration	M							
No Booking (2 yrs)	D							
Charge Bar Expenditure				I				
Amend Bar Charge				M				
Bar Tariff Change				M				
Charge Rest, Expend					I			
Amend Rest. Charge					M			
Restaurant Tariff Change					M			
Day Start						I		
Day End						D		
Structural Alter.			M			M	M	M/I/D
Room Tariff Change								M
Overbooking Change						M		
Archive Bar Charge				D				
Archive Rest Charge					D			
Archive Booking		D						
Archive Occupancy			D					

Appendix 4 Entity/ Event Matrix

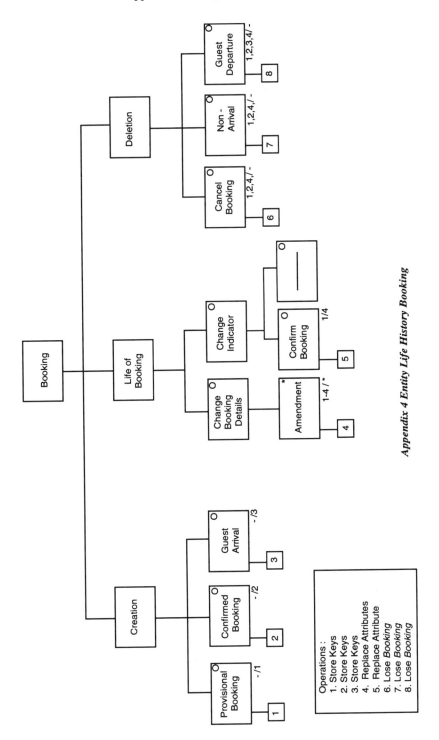

Appendix 4 Entity Life History Booking

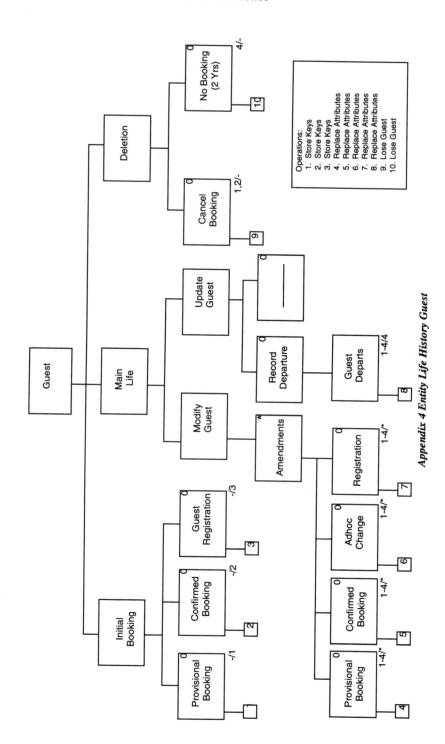

Appendix 4 Entity Life History Guest

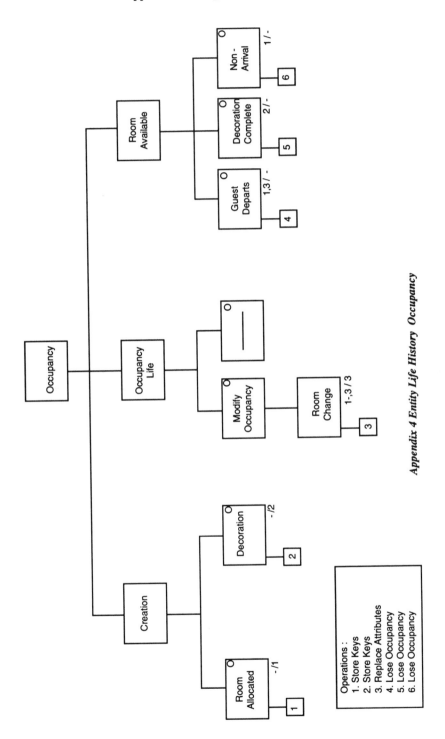

Appendix 4 Entity Life History Occupancy

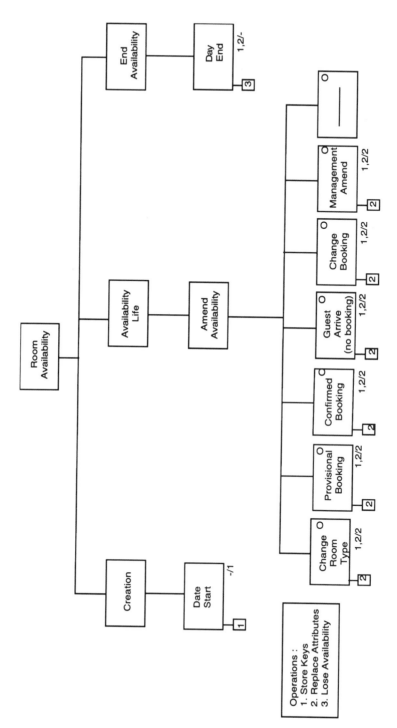

Appendix 4 Entity Life History Room Availability

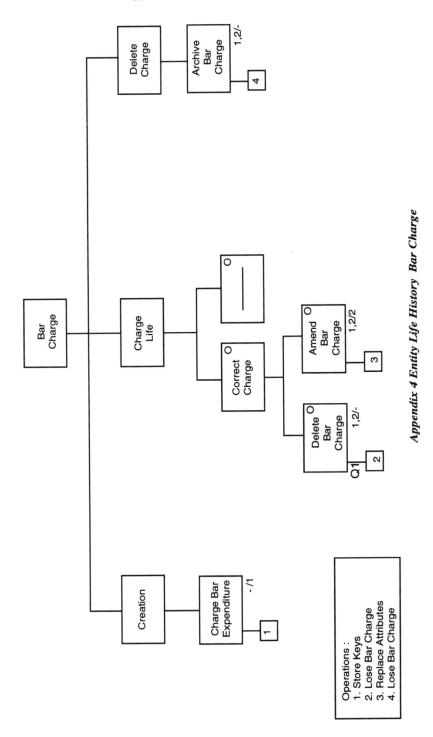

Appendix 4 Entity Life History Bar Charge

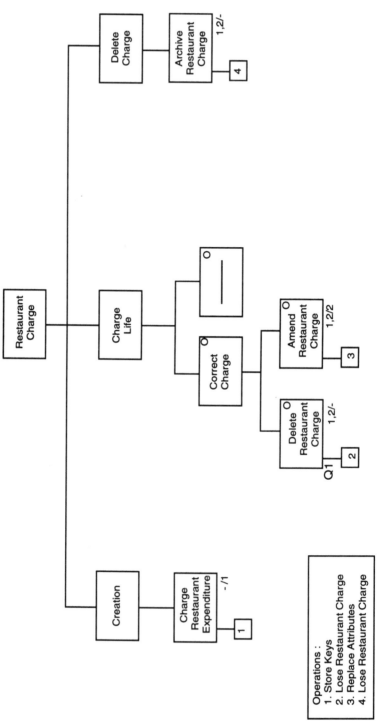

Appendix 4 Entity Life History Restaurant Charge

Operations :
1. Store Keys
2. Lose Restaurant Charge
3. Replace Attributes
4. Lose Restaurant Charge

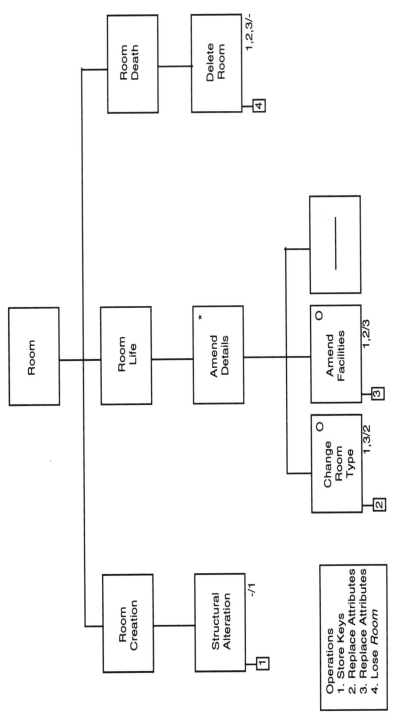

Appendix 4 Entity Life History Room

Room

Room
Life

Room
Creation

Room
Death

Structural
Alteration

Amend
Details *

Delete
Room

Change
Room
Type O

Amend
Facilities O

-/1

1,2,3/-

1,3/2

1,2/3

Operations
1. Store Keys
2. Replace Attributes
3. Replace Attributes
4. Lose *Room*

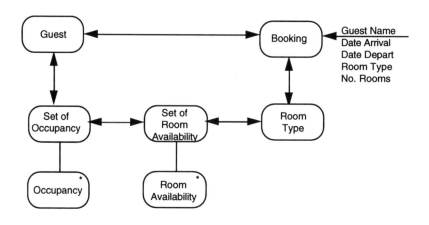

Appendix 4 Effect Correspondence Diagram - Cancel Booking

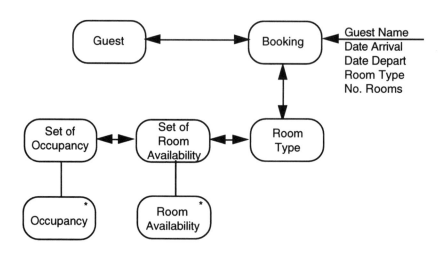

*Appendix 4 Effect Correspondence Diagram - Change Booking, Non-arrival
and Room Allocated*

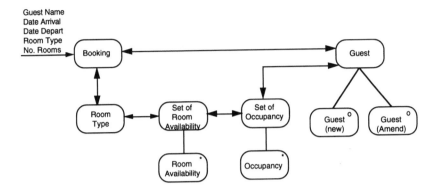

Appendix 4 Effect Correspondence Diagram - Guest Arival (No booking)

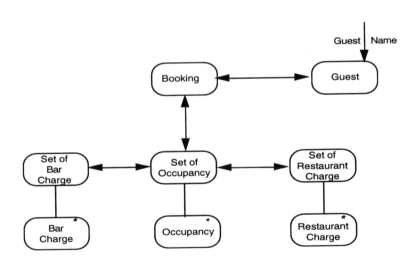

Appendix 4 Effect Correspondence Diagram - Guest Departs

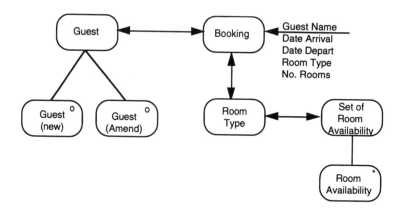

Appendix 4 Effect Correspondence Diagram - Provisional/Confirmed Booking

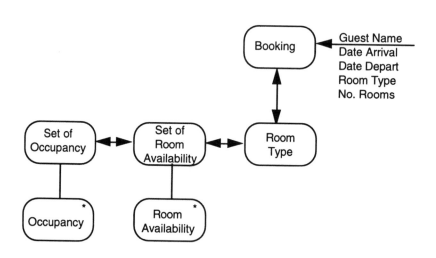

Appendix 4 Effect Correspondence Diagram - Room Change

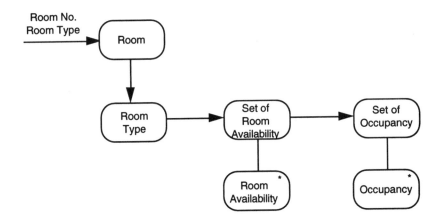

Appendix 4 Effect Correspondence Diagram - Structural Alteration,
Decoration and Decoration Complete

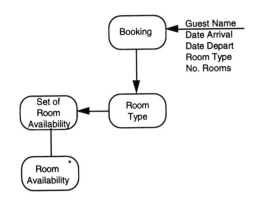

Appendix 4 Enquiry Access Path - Booking Enquiry, Room Change, Guest
Arrival (no booking) and Change Booking

Appendix 5 - Stage 5 Products

Stage 5 is the Logical Design Stage of the system development. This is very much a stage where information in the products of Stage 4 is collected together and used to construct the Logical Design.

Much of this work is repetiative; the products supplied in the appendix are a set of examples of the various diagrams and supporting text that would be required to document a complete project.

Included are the products that provide the menu structure and details for the Receptionist, the Enhanced Effect Correspondence Diagrams that are used to construct the Update Process Structures and two examples of the Operations Lists and Update Process Structures that should be produced from these. There is also an Enhanced Enquiry Access Path diagram and the resultant products.

Dialogue Element Description : Receptionist/Accounts			
Dialogue Element	**Data Item**	**LGDE**	**M/O**
Departures Due	Date Guest_Surname Guest_Forenames Room_No	DEP_1	M/O
Accommodation Details	Guest_Surname Guest_Forenames Guest_Address Room_No Room_Type Tariff No_nights Accomm_Charge	BILL_1	M
Occupancy Details	Room_No Bar_Charges Rest_Charges	BILL_2	M
Special Rate Details	Special_Rate	BILL_3	O
Total Bill Details	Date Guest_Surname Guest_Forenames Guest_Address Room_No Room_Type No_nights Accomm_Charge Bar_Charge_Total Rest_Charge_Total Discount Total_Charge	BILL_4	M

Appendix 5 Dialogue Element Description - Guest Departs

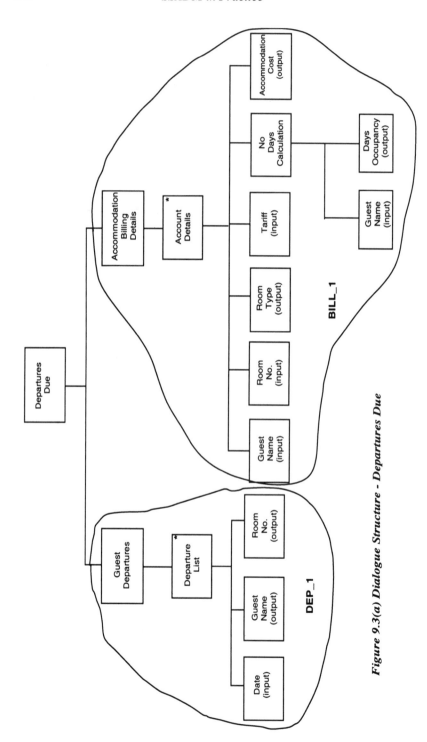

Figure 9.3(a) Dialogue Structure - Departures Due

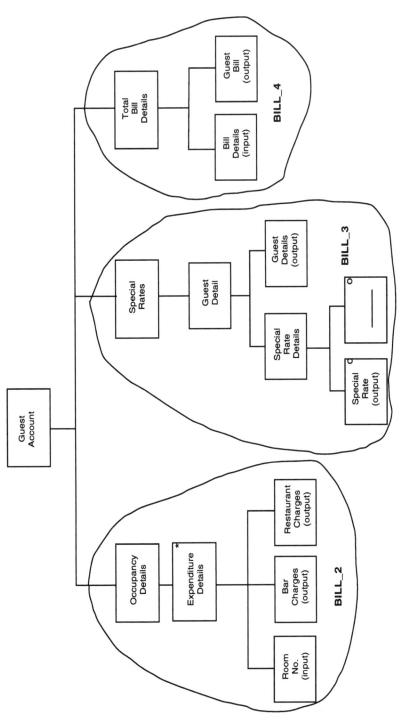

Figure 9.3(b) Dialogue Structure - Guest Accounts

Command Control Structure : Receptionist/Accounts		
Option	**Dialogue or Menu**	**Dialogue/Menu Name**
Daily Departures	Menu	Accounts
Departure List	Menu	Daily Departures
Departures Due	Dialogue	DEP-1
Quit to Menu	Menu	Daily Departures
Charge Accommodation	Menu	Daily Departures
Accommodation Details	Dialogue	BILL_1
Quit to Menu	Menu	Acounts
Expenditure Charges	Menu	Accounts
Occupancy Details	Dialogue	BILL_2
Special Rate Details	Dialogue	BILL_3
Quit to Menu	Menu	Accounts
Finalise Account	Menu	Accounts
Final Bill Details	Dialogue	BILL_4
Quit to Menu	Menu	Accounts

Appendix 5 Command Control Structure - Guest Departs

Dialogue Element Description : Receptionist/Allocation			
Dialogue Element	**Data Item**	**LGDE**	**M/O**
Arrivals	Date Guest_Surname Guest_Forenames Date_Arrive Date_depart Room_Type No_Rooms No_Guests	ARR_1	M
Allocate Room	Guest_Surname Guest_Forenames Special Requirements Date_Arrive Date_depart Room_Type No_Rooms No_Guests Room_No	ALLOC_1	M
Arrivals List	Date Guest_Surname Guest_Forenames Date_Arrive Room_No	ARR_2	M

Appendix 5 Dialogue Element Description - Allocation

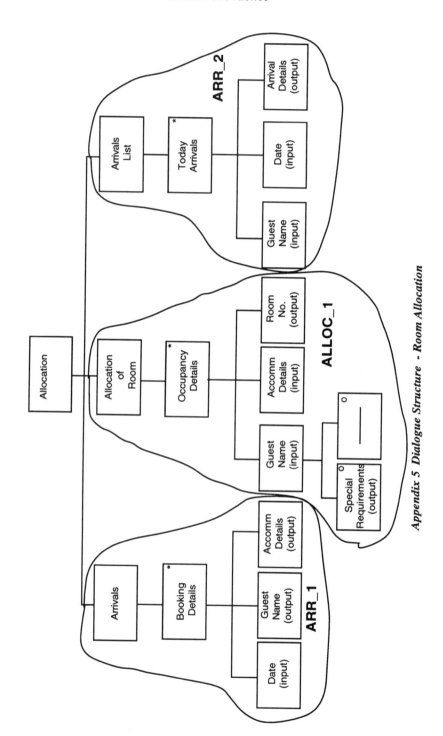

Appendix 5 Dialogue Structure - Room Allocation

Command Control Structure : Receptionist/Allocation		
Option	**Dialogue or Menu**	**Dialogue/Menu Name**
Daily Arrivals	Menu	Arrivals
Arrival Details	Dialogue	ARR_1
Allocation	Dialogue	ALLOC_1
Quit to Menu	Menu	Arrivals
Arrivals List	Dialogue	ARR_2
Quit to Menu	Menu	Reception

Appendix 5 Command Control Structure - Allocation

Dialogue Element Description : Receptionist/Registration			
Dialogue Element	**Data Item**	**LGDE**	**M/O**
Partial Registration	Date Guest_Surname Guest_Forenames Guest_Address Guest_Phone Company Special Requirements Date_Last_Stay Number_Stays Special_Discount	REG_1	M
Identification Card	Guest_Surname Guest_Forenames Room_No Room_Type Date_Arrival	REG_2	M
Complete Registration	Car_Reg Method_Payment Nationality Passport_no Issued_At Destination	REG_3	M

Appendix 5 Dialogue Element Description - Registration of Guest

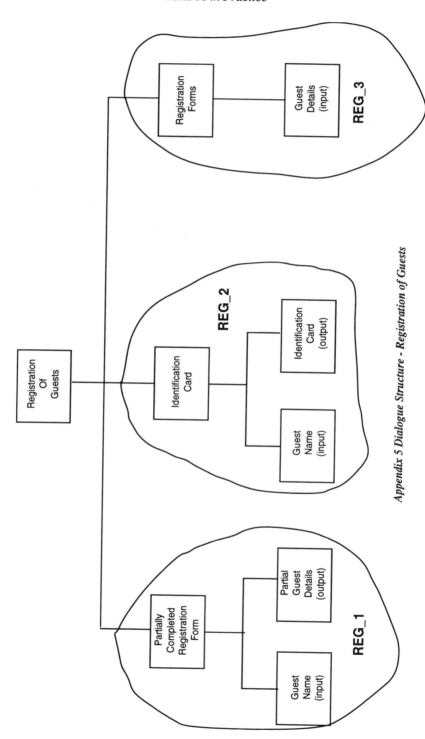

Appendix 5 Dialogue Structure - Registration of Guests

Command Control Structure : Receptionist/Accounts		
Option	**Dialogue or Menu**	**Dialogue/Menu Name**
Registration	Menu	Registration
Partial Registration	Dialogue	REG_1
Quit to Menu	Menu	Registration
Identification Card	Dialogue	REG_2
Quit to Menu	Menu	Registration
Complete Registration	Dialogue	REG_3
Quit to Menu	Menu	Reception

Appendix 5 Command Control Structure - Registration

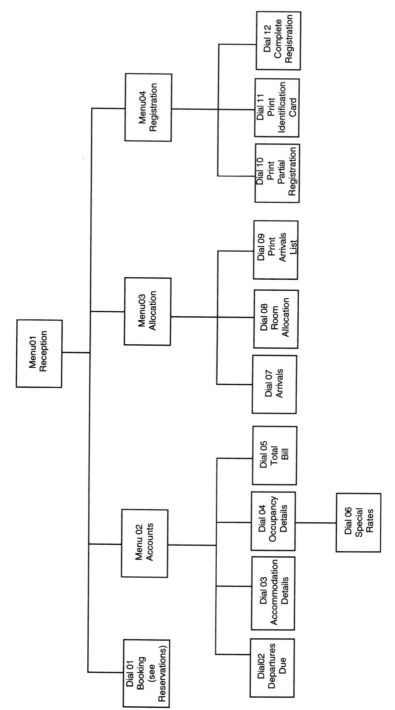

Appendix 5 Menu Structure - Receptionist

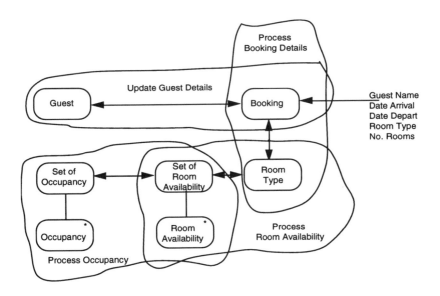

Appendix 5 Enhanced Effect Correspondence Diagram - Cancel Booking

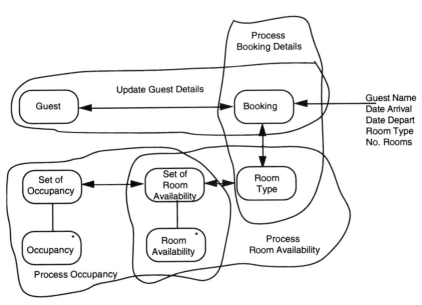

Appendix 5 Enhanced Effect Correspondence Diagram - Change Booking,
Non-Arrival and Room Allocated

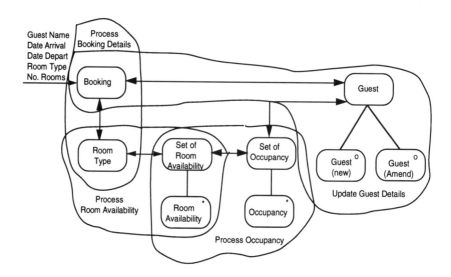

Appendix 5 Enhanced Effect Correspondence Diagram - Guest Arrival (No Booking)

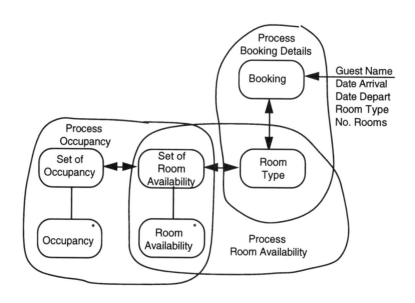

Appendix 5 Enhanced Effect Correspondence Diagram - Room Change

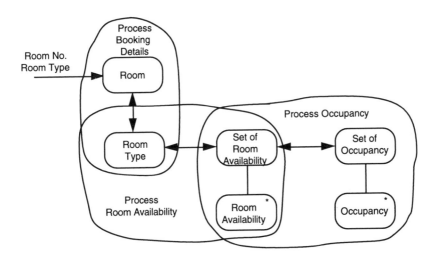

Appendix 5 Enhanced Effect Correspondence Diagram - Structural Alteration, Decoration and Decoration complete

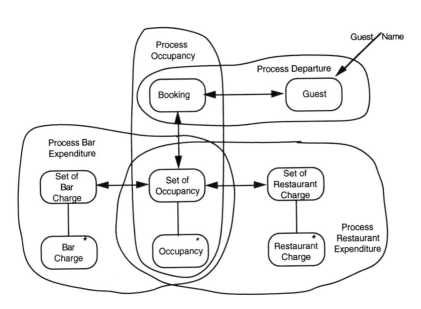

Figure 9.5 Enhanced Effect Correspondence Diagram - Guest Departs

Appendix 5 Enhanced Effect Correspondence Diagram - Guest Departs

Operations List - Update Process Sructure : Guest Departs

1. Read *Guest* by *key*
2. Fail if SI <> 1- 4
3. Store *attribute*
4. Write *Guest*
5. Read *Booking* by *key*
6. Fail if SI <> 1 - 4
    7. Read *Occupancy* by *key*
    8. Fail if SI <> 1,2
        9. Read *Bar Charge*s by *key*
        10. Fail if SI <> 1,2
        11. Read *Archive Bar Charge* by *key*
        12. Fail if SI <> null
        13. Create *Archive Bar Charge*
        14. Store *attribute*s
        15. Write *Archive Bar Charge*
        16. Delete *Bar Charge*
        17. Read *Restaurant Charge* by *key*
        18. Fail if SI <> 1,2
        19. Read *Archive Restaurant Charge* by *key*
        20. Fail if SI <> null
        21. Create *Archive Restaurant Charge*
        22. Store *attribute*s
        23. Write *Archive Restaurant Charge*
        24. Delete *Restaurant Charge*
    25. Read *Archive Occupancy*
    26. Fail if SI <> null
    27. Create *Archive Occupancy*
    28. Store *attribute*s
    29. Write *Archive Occupancy*
    30. Delete *Occupancy*
31. Read *Archive Booking* by *key*
32. Fail if SI <> null
33. Create *Archive Booking*
34. Store *attribute*s
35. Write *Archive Booking*
36. Delete *Booking*

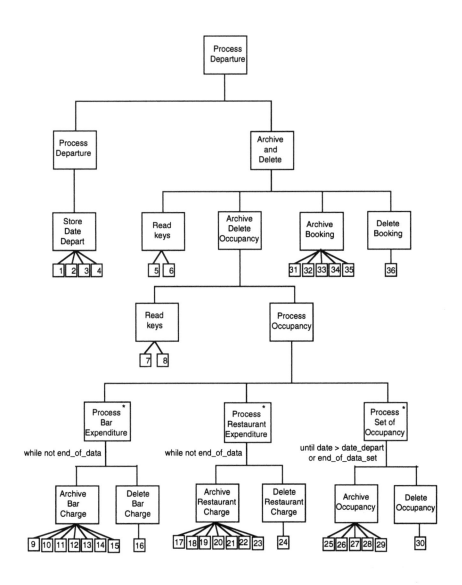

Appendix 5 Update Process Structure - Guest Departs

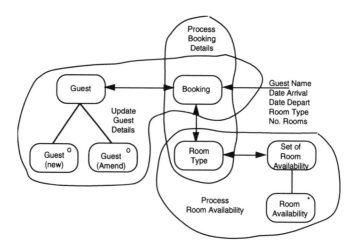

*Appendix 5 Enhanced Effect Correspondence Diagram - Provisional/
Confirmed Booking*

Operations List - Update Process Structure : Provisional/Confirmed Booking

1. Read *Booking* by *key*
2. Fail if SI <> null
3. Create *Booking*
4. Store *attribute*
5. Read *Guest* by *key*
6. Fail if SI <> null
7. Create *Guest*
8. Store *attribute*s
9. Write *Guest*
10. Read *Guest* by *key*
11. Fail if SI <> 1-4
12. Store *attributes*
13. Write *Guest*
        14. Read *Room Availability* by *key*
        15. Fail if SI <> 1,2
        16. Calculate *Room Available* using *No_rooms*
        17. Store *attributes*
        18. Write *Room Availability*
19. Write *Booking*

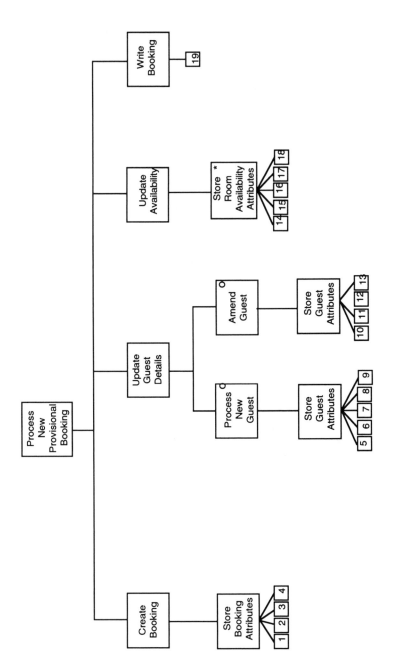

Appendix 5 Update Process Structure - New Provisional Booking

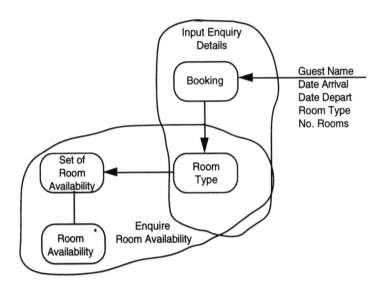

Appendix 5 Enhanced Enquiry Access Path - Booking Enquiry

Operations List -   Enquiry Process Sructure :
                        Booking Enquiry

1. Read *Room Type* by *key*
2. Fail if SI <> 1,2
                          3. Read *Room Availability* by *key*
                          4. Fail if (room_available - No_Rooms) < 0

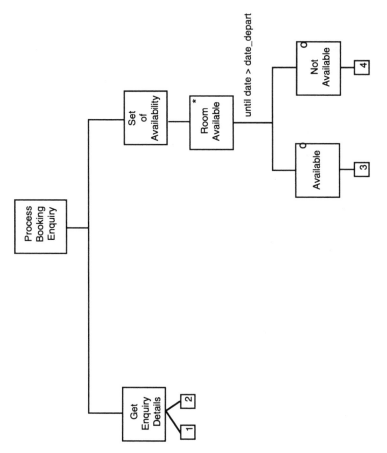

Enquiry Process Structure - Booking Enquiry

Appendix 6 - Physical Design

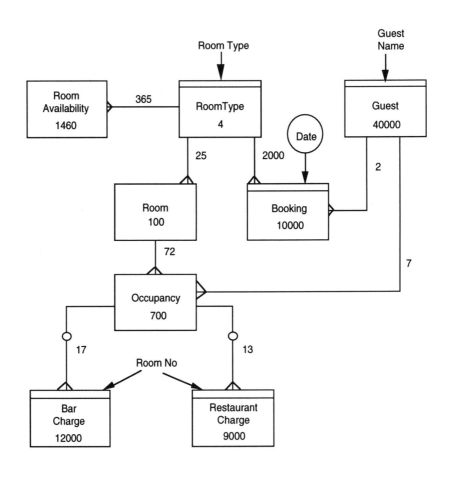

Appendix 6 Physical Data Structure

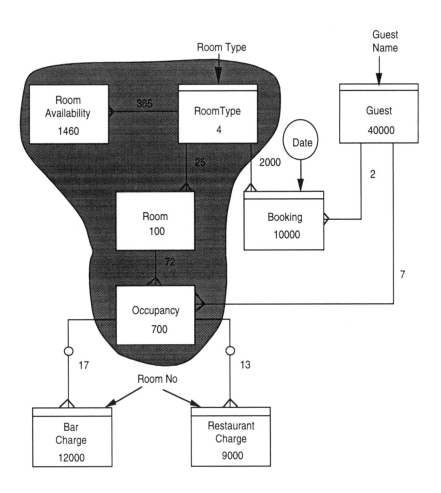

Appendix 6 Physical Data Structure

Appendix 7- Requirements Catalogue

The Requirements Catalogue is an ongoing document that is referred to and updated throughout the life of the project. The information is originally collated in Stage 1; in the Case Study example the catalogue is in some areas complete and in others has yet to be correctly updated.

Requirements Catalogue

System : *Hotel*	Variant :	
Functional Requirement : *Advanced Booking, up to twelve months*	Owner :	**Require. ID** 1
	Priority : *1*	

Non-Functional Requirement(s)

Description	Target Value	Acceptable Range	Comments

Benefits :
> *Increased level of customer service*
> *Advance knowledge of demand*

Comments/Suggested Solutions :
> *Room availability Entity with 365 occurrences, occurrence deleted at 'end of day' and a new occurrence created (365 days in advance) at 'end of day'*

Related Documents :
> *Reservations Diary*

Related Requirements :

Resolution :

Requirements Catalogue

System : *Hotel*		Variant :	

Functional Requirement : *Up to Date and Accurate recording* *of expenditure*	Owner :	Require. ID 2
	Priority : *1*	

Non-Functional Requirement(s)

Description	Target Value	Acceptable Range	Comments
Frequency of *entry of* *expenditure data*	*Immediately a* *transaction is* *completed*	*Immediately a* *transaction is* *completed*	
Data Back_Up	*At end of each* *opening session in* *Bar and restaurant*	*Daily*	

Benefits :
> *Minimise Bill Amendments*
> *Customer Satisfaction*

Comments/Suggested Solutions :
Use of Point of Sale Terminals in Bar and Restaurant

Related Documents :
Chitties, Standard Tariff, Customer Records

Related Requirements :

Resolution :
Identification issued to Guests on Registration, to be used when charges made .
Charges entered by Bar/Restaurant Personnel using POS terminals and Room
No. as key.

Requirements Catalogue			
System : *Hotel*		**Variant :**	
Functional Requirement : *Specific Room Requests for advance booking*		**Owner :**	**Require. ID** *3*
		Priority : *1*	

Non-Functional Requirement(s)

Description	Target Value	Acceptable Range	Comments

Benefits :

    Customer Service

Comments/Suggested Solutions :

Rooms normally allocated on day of arrival; however, guests may request a specific room and this is noted in the booking details

Related Documents :

Reservations Diary, Room Chart

Related Requirements :

Booking 12 months in advance

Resolution :

Booking occurrence to include special requests, this will be checked on allocation of room

Requirements Catalogue

System :	Hotel	Variant :		

Functional Requirement :
Customer Records Live for 2 years after last booking

Owner :	Require. ID	4
Priority : 1		

Non-Functional Requirement(s)

Description	Target Value	Acceptable Range	Comments
Deletion of old customer records	*deleted two years after last departure date*	*deleted in the month, 2years after last departure date*	

Benefits :
More efficient for Guest Detail searches

Comments/Suggested Solutions :
Include Last_Departure_Date field in Guest details

Related Documents :
Customer Details

Related Requirements :

Resolution :
Monthly search through Guest details on Last_Departure_Date, delete any occurrence older than two years.

Requirements Catalogue

System : *Hotel*	Variant :	

Functional Requirement : *Bills produced in 2 minutes*	Owner :	Require. ID 5
	Priority : *1*	

Non-Functional Requirement(s)

Description	Target Value	Acceptable Range	Comments
Bills produced in 2 minutes	*Bills produced in 2 minutes*	*Bills produced in 2 minutes*	

Benefits :

Customer Satisfaction
Greater Accuracy as bill raised as guest signs out, allowing inclusion of any last minute expenditure.

Comments/Suggested Solutions :

Related Documents :

Chitties, Customer Records, Standard Tariff, Departure List

Related Requirements :

Accuracy of charges

Resolution :

Automation of collection of relevant data from Bar, Restaurant and Occupancy
Automatic calculation of totals using standard tariff details

Requirements Catalogue

System : *Hotel*	Variant :

Functional Requirement : *Reservation Data continuously available*	Owner :	Require. ID 6

	Priority : *1*	

Non-Functional Requirement(s)

Description	Target Value	Acceptable Range	Comments
Ability to access reservation data at all times	*reservation service available 24 hours a day*	*reservation service available 24 hours a day*	

Benefits :
Accurate Assessment of staffing levels
Marketing information
Ability to provide customer information and booking at any time day or night

Comments/Suggested Solutions :
On-line enquiry into booking information
That reservations remains a role but can be carried out by any clerical staff member

Related Documents :
Reservation Diary

Related Requirements :

Resolution :

Requirements Catalogue

System : *Hotel*	Variant :		

Functional Requirement :
Facility for Management to overbook

Owner :	Require. ID 7
Priority : *2*	

Non-Functional Requirement(s)

Description	Target Value	Acceptable Range	Comments
Management only access for setting the overbooking percentages			

Benefits :
   Cancellation would not always adversely affect occupancy levels

Comments/Suggested Solutions :
   Overbooking Field in Room Availability

Related Documents :
   Reservation Diary, Room Chart

Related Requirements :

Resolution :
   Provide access to the Room Availability, through the Maintenance function to allow update of the overbooking field

Requirements Catalogue

System : *Hotel*	Variant :	

Functional Requirement : *Facility to designate rooms as unavailable for determined and undetermined periods*	Owner :	Require. ID *8*
	Priority : *1*	

Non-Functional Requirement(s)

Description	Target Value	Acceptable Range	Comments
management only access			

Benefits :
    A room can be taken out of commission for decoration (undetermined period) or for management use (determined)

Comments/Suggested Solutions :
    Access for management to Room Availability and Occupancy to enable room being classified as booked

Related Documents :
Reservation Diary, Room Chart

Related Requirements :

Resolution :

Requirements Catalogue

System : *Hotel*	Variant :	

Functional Requirement : *Accurate , fast and cheap* *Management Information*	Owner :	Require. ID 9
	Priority : 2	

Non-Functional Requirement(s)

Description	Target Value	Acceptable Range	Comments
management only access *provision of occupancy and customer analysis*	*Information on demand*	*24 hours*	

Benefits : *Accuracy in staffing levels*
        Marketing needs
        Budgeting
        Maintenance

Comments/Suggested Solutions :

Related Documents :
  Reservation Diary, Room Chart, Customer File

Related Requirements :

Resolution :

Requirements Catalogue

System : *Hotel*		Variant :	

Functional Requirement : *Information of arrivals and departures to reach housekeeper before morning cleaning routines are planned*	**Owner :**	**Require. ID** *10*
	Priority : *1*	

Non-Functional Requirement(s)

Description	Target Value	Acceptable Range	Comments
Task initiated by Reception, automated procedure	*Once a day, before 6am*	*Once a day, before 6am*	

Benefits :   *Efficient Allocation of Domestic Staff*
Minimise inconvenience to Guests

Comments/Suggested Solutions :

Related Documents :

Reservation Diary, Room Chart, Arrivals List, Departure List

Related Requirements :

Resolution :

Requirements Catalogue			
System : *Hotel*		**Variant :**	
Functional Requirement : *Eliminate Errors in calculation of rooms available*		**Owner :**	**Require. ID** *11*
		Priority : *1*	

Non-Functional Requirement(s)

Description	Target Value	Acceptable Range	Comments

Benefits : *Customer Satisfaction*
Accurate Staffing Level Assessment
Ability to plan maintenance

Comments/Suggested Solutions :

Related Documents :

Reservation Diary, Room Chart

Related Requirements :

Resolution :
Automatic amendment of rooms available levels on receipt of initial booking and any subsequent alterations

Requirements Catalogue			
System : *Hotel*		Variant :	
Functional Requirement : *Accuracy of allocation of Bar/Restaurant charges to correct guest*		Owner :	Require. ID *12*
		Priority : *1*	
Non-Functional Requirement(s)			

Description	Target Value	Acceptable Range	Comments

Benefits :   *Customer Satisfaction*
               Accuracy of billing

Comments/Suggested Solutions :

Related Documents :

   Bar Chitties, Restaurant Bills

Related Requirements :

Resolution :
Identification Cards to be used for Authorisation, Room Number entered on POS terminal as key to transaction

Index

263